It's me or the dog

HYPERION

NEW YORK

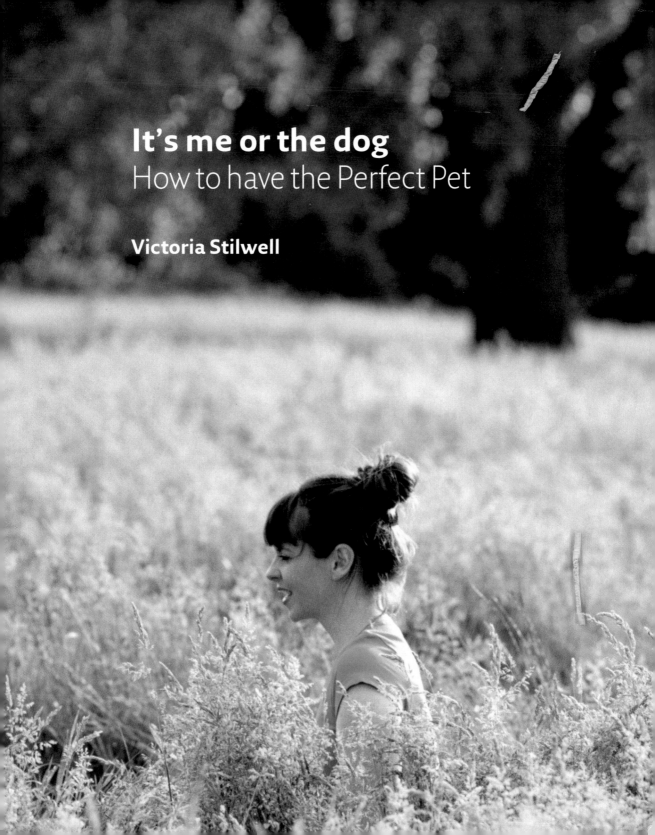

It's me or the dog
How to have the Perfect Pet

Victoria Stilwell

I dedicate this book to my beloved
husband Van and daughter Alexandra.
I am blessed to have you in my life and
love you both so much.

Text copyright © 2005, 2007 Ricochet
Photography copyright © 2005, 2007 Mark Read

First published in Great Britain in 2005 by Collins, an imprint of HarperCollins
Publishers

ISBN: 1-4013-0855-4 / 978-1-4013-0855-1

Hyperion books are available for special promotions and premiums. For details
contact Michael Rentas, Assistant Director, Inventory Operations, Hyperion,
77 West 66th Street, 12th floor, New York, New York 10023, or call 212-456-0133.

First U.S. Edition
10   9   8   7   6   5   4   3   2   1

Note: Dogs are referred to as "he" throughout this book. This is no reflection of
gender bias but was simply intended to make things easier for the reader. I see
dogs of both sexes in my work, and the techniques outlined in the following
pages will work whether your dog is a "he" or a "she."

Contents

Introduction

When I was a child, I longed for a dog. I used to put notes under my father's pillow at night. "Please Daddy, can I have a dog? I promise you that if I get a dog I will never be naughty again." My father always refused. There was one important reason why, and it was not the fact that he was not a dog-lover himself. Instead, it was because he knew that after the novelty wore off, he and my mother would be the ones who would have to look after the animal. As they both worked, it simply wasn't practical. Looking back, I know they were right. In the last 15 years, I've more than made up for lost time. I've been a professional dog-walker, I've worked at dog shelters and in dogs' homes, and continue to advise various rescue organizations. And I've fostered more than 40 dogs that were too old, too difficult, or too sick to be easily re-homed.

When I was growing up, the closest I came to owning a dog was to visit the Beagles my grandmother bred. Our favorite outing was to walk the dogs along the fields beside the River Thames. Occasionally, the dogs would make a run for freedom. I have lasting memories of four Beagles taking off into the sunset, ears flapping, mouths turned up in grins at the thrill of the chase, while my grandmother, to no avail, yelled at them to come back. They were the worst-trained dogs you could imagine, but when they eventually returned home by themselves a couple of hours later, dirty, tired, and exhilarated, they were the happiest creatures on earth.

My grandmother was a great inspiration to me, and has been a huge influence on my work. She grew up in a privileged, well-to-do home, with four older brothers, but she never conformed to how her father expected his little girl to behave. Rather than wearing pretty dresses, she longed to ride horses, work in kennels, and get muddy and dirty like her brothers were allowed to do. When her father died while she was in her teens, she proceeded to go her own way. Well before I came on the scene, she set up one of the first dog-grooming parlors in London, and then she became a breeder of Beagles. Her dogs, while a little lacking in training, were never spoiled, but they always came first in her affections. Those dogs had a five-star lifestyle.

Benno was my first dog. I say "my," but he wasn't really mine. I was a young aspiring actor, and like many actors, was spending more time waiting tables than appearing on the stage. My sister was a veterinary nurse who supplemented her income by taking occasional dog-sitting jobs. Flat broke, and desperate to lead some semblance of a normal life, I took her advice and advertised myself as a dog-sitter. Within days, I received my first call, from Benno's owners.

Benno was a Border Collie puppy who lived with two busy lawyers. Even then, it seemed strange to me that two people who were working all day had decided to bring a puppy into their home, but at least they had the good sense to employ someone to care for him while they were out.

I will never forget our first walk on Wimbledon Common. Benno looked up at me with such excitement, and somehow his eyes conveyed an energy that flowed right through me. That moment marked the beginning of my wonderful relationship with dogs.

Within a couple of months of taking that first job walking Benno, I was exercising 20 dogs a day. The morning shift consisted of what I called the "misfits," a motley crew representing many of the more popular breeds. Teddy, the Labrador puppy, was only too happy to roll in every patch of mud he could find. Shanty, the epileptic Bearded Collie, liked to leap over ferns like a would-be Giselle, while Wilbur, the white Boxer, who pretended to be the tough guy, was always the first one to run and hide behind my legs when any of the other dogs got angry with him.

The afternoon shift comprised the "aristocrats": The Schnauzer, Willie, and Archie, the West Highland Terrier, looked down their noses at all the other dogs, while delicately sniffing the ground around them. However, Jessie, the German Shepherd, whose owner was a well-known politician, kept everyone in their place.

Whether with misfits or aristocrats, I would walk for hours on Wimbledon Common surrounded by these glorious creatures. The dogs never ran away, even though they were off the leash, nor did they fight. I never questioned why they didn't. It wasn't until I became a trainer that I understood why those dogs wanted to be with me.

To the dogs, I was their leader and they listeneed to everything I said. They knew that they had a good thing going, and that when I showed up to walk them, pleasant and exciting things were about to happen. They respected me because I treated them with the utmost care and respect. They trusted me and knew that I was their protector. Those dogs with their quirks and diverse personalities were my introduction into the fascinating world of canine behavior.

One day on the Common I met a behaviorist and we got talking. By then, I was becoming more curious about why dogs acted the way that they did, and from that point onward I began to back up my observations with study, reading books, going to seminars, and taking courses. At the same time, I volunteered as a walker for the famous Battersea Dogs' Home – my first experience of handling rescue dogs. I also worked with Greyhound rescue agencies and other dog shelters.

When I moved across the Atlantic to New York City in 1999, my work stepped up a notch. I set up a training school to instruct families with children on safe and effective dog training. I worked with the ASPCA and with rescue shelters in Manhattan. Now I train dogs all over New York, New Jersey, and Pennsylvania, and serve as a behavior adviser to a number of rescue organizations in the same tri-state area.

Over the past five years, my husband and I have also fostered many dogs that would not otherwise have found a home. We look after the old ones until they die, and nurture the ones who require medication or who have been seriously abused. In many cases, we have been able to rehabilitate dogs who have been abandoned or ill-treated, and find them new homes. Some of the dogs stay only a couple of weeks before they move on to a new home; some stay a year or more.

The two sides of my work, dog rescue and dog training, are deeply linked. Do you know that 96% of dogs that end up abandoned in shelters have never had any training? The year before I arrived in New York, 67,000 dogs and cats found themselves in shelters, and 47,000 of them were put down. That's a tragic waste of life. The situation has now improved somewhat, with owners becoming more aware of the need to neuter their pets, but more dogs are still being bred than there are people who are willing to look after them properly.

I have a profound respect for the domestic dog. For thousands of years, the dog has cohabited with humans, and put up with all the idiosyncrasies of our world. This unique and unbreakable partnership between dog and human has made the dog one of the most successful species on the planet. Your dog's predecessors ensured the survival of the species by aligning themselves with the one other species that has the utmost power to protect them from threat: man. From fighting a constant battle for survival in the wild to sleeping on a comfy couch with an endless supply of food and affection – now that's a clever animal!

When I ask a new client what they want to achieve by training their dog, the standard response is that they want to train their dog to be obedient. They want their dog to respond to commands, such as "sit," "get down," and "stay," to be house-trained, and to get along with other people and other dogs.

Then I ask them: What do they think their dog needs? The reply is always very similar. Clients usually say that their dog needs to learn to "sit," "stay," and "get down," to be house-trained, and to behave. And that is the popular view of what dog training is all about.

What I hardly ever hear is that a client wants to learn how their dog learns, how their dog communicates, and what their dog needs in order to be successful. But that's just it – training is about understanding how your dog perceives the world around him. Using this knowledge, you can then become a better communicator and create an environment where your dog is happy and has the confidence to cope with domestic life. Understanding and communication: It's as simple as that. We're so focused on getting our dogs to sit, stay, and come when called that we lose the very reason *why* we are doing this.

This book is all about giving you a solid foundation of knowledge on which to build your training. Think of it as your support system. Of course, you can teach your dog to "sit" and to "come" without understanding much about his innate behavior. But sooner or later you will run into a problem or an area of difficulty that demands a more subtle approach. If you don't understand what makes a dog tick, or how to communicate with him in a language that he can understand, you won't be able to solve the problem.

And at this point, many owners respond in one of two ways: Either they give up and ignore the situation, or they resort to harsh punishment that inevitably makes things worse. Some people carry on living their lives with an unruly pet, accepting all the restrictions that this state of affairs imposes upon them. Others find themselves at the end of their wits and decide to give up their dog. It doesn't have to be that way.

As a trainer, I've seen it all, from the dog who tried to eat through a wall every time his owner left the house, to more common problems, such as chewing shoes, barking in the garden, and chasing cats. As a dog fosterer, I know only too well what price pets pay when their owners can't or won't train them properly. That's why I was delighted to be asked to take part in the television series *It's Me or the Dog*, and show how fundamentally simple techniques can really turn around what seem like hopeless situations.

Throughout the book, you will find advice on every aspect of caring for dogs, from what to feed them to how to walk them. At the same time, you'll also find tried and tested solutions to the type of common problems most dog-owners encounter from time to time. Training isn't about imposing your will on your dog; it's about giving him the tools he needs to live in your world.

Dogs are amazing animals. They never cease to fascinate and inspire me. Take the time to train your pet and you will be rewarded many times over by the love, affection, and sheer good company that dogs bring into our lives.

My top ten rules for raising and training a dog

1 Think dog
Understand how dogs learn and what makes them tick as a species. Dogs are not humans, but many people treat them like they are.

2 Talk dog
Learn how to communicate effectively in *dog* language. Dogs can't speak English, or any other human language. You, however, can learn to talk dog.

3 Top dog
Who's in charge? You are. You have to be your dog's pack leader. He'll be much happier and better behaved if he has an effective leader to follow.

4 Accentuate the positive
Reward good behavior. Good things happen when your dog does well! Ignore or correct behavior you don't want to encourage. Sounds simple, but many people do exactly the opposite without meaning to. Never, ever use harsh punishment.

5 Perfect timing
Get the timing right when rewarding or correcting. Dogs won't associate a reward or correction with an action if you leave it too long to respond. You need to give feedback within *one second* of the behavior.

6 He says, she says
Be consistent at all times – and that goes for everyone in the family. Use the same commands and agree on your house rules. Can the dog sit on the sofa or not? Mixed messages confuse dogs and make them anxious because they can't work out what they're supposed to do.

7 Know your dog
Your dog is an individual with his own strengths and weaknesses, likes and dislikes. Whether he's purebred or a mixed breed, there are breed characteristics to take into account, too. Go with the flow.

8 Vary the picture
Offer a variety of different experiences to stimulate your dog's brain and senses. Dogs like to play and they get bored, just like we do. Don't just train in the same place or using the same posture. Teach your dog to respond to you in every situation.

9 Lifelong learning
Start training early and keep reinforcing the learning all through the dog's life. You can, and should, teach an old dog new tricks.

10 Easy does it
Make it easy for your dog to do well and succeed. Manage his environment. Put the shoes away so he can't chew them. When you're training your dog, accept failure as part of the learning process. Successful training requires patience.

Think Dog understanding your dog

In order to train your dog, you first have to see the world from his point of view. Dogs aren't human beings, but many people treat them as if they were – and the problems start right there. Your dog may be living with humans in a human world, but his instincts remain pure dog.

Let's take one example. You take your dog to the park, he runs around for a while, sniffing the ground, and then he stops and rolls in the grass. If you see the scene through human eyes, you assume the dog is rolling in the grass for the sheer pleasure of it. Maybe you think he's found a new way to scratch his back. Both interpretations may be partially correct, but it's also likely that he is rolling in the grass to cover himself in a particular, appealing scent (and one that you probably can't even smell). Experts aren't entirely sure, but it is thought that wolves cover themselves in scent to reinforce their status within the pack, or to disguise their own scent when hunting prey.

That's a simple example of misunderstanding dog behavior, and one that has no particular impact on your relationship with your dog. In many other circumstances, however, getting the signals wrong can give rise to more serious problems. Understanding how a dog learns and how he perceives the world will provide you with a solid foundation upon which to base your training, and a means of communicating effectively with your pet .

Your dog may be
living with humans
in a human world,
but his instincts
remain pure dog.

The pack

Dogs and people are able to live together so successfully because in some ways the two species are very similar. Like us, dogs are social creatures. In the wild, the wolf, the domestic dog's ancestor, lives in packs composed of extended family groups. It nurtures its young for a relatively long period, and it communicates with its pack members using a wide range of signals – both gestures and sounds. The pack is structured in a clear order or hierarchy, with a dominant male and female pair at the top of the group and other members ranked lower down, depending on age, sex, and abilities.

Communication is vital for the survival of the pack. It allows members to coordinate attacks on prey, and it plays a key role in establishing bonds within the group. Just as important, it reinforces the pecking order so that each pack member knows its place in the scheme of things. Many people wrongly assume that if left to their own devices, dogs would constantly fight for control and dominance. The reverse is actually true. Violence is an exception in wild dog or wolf behavior; deference is the norm. In fact, the hierarchy in packs is expressly designed to prevent the disruption of fighting, as well as to ensure that in times of crisis, the strongest survives to the benefit of the species as a whole.

Why you have to be top dog

When you bring a puppy or dog into your home, your family becomes his pack. That begs the question: Who is pack leader? The answer is: It has to be you.

You are your dog's guide to the weird and wonderful domestic environment in which he finds himself. Dogs may have been human companions for thousands of years, but that does not make it any easier for them to live by your rules without clear direction. When you are the leader, the dog will take his cues from you and settle much more confidently into your home.

Some breeds of dog are naturally more dominant than others, as are some individual dogs. But all dogs are much happier and better behaved when they recognize their human owners are in control. They're happier because they are free of the stress of being in charge. They're better behaved because they know that if all the good things in life come through you – including food, toys, praise, petting, and attention – you become a valuable source and your dog is more likely to listen and respect you.

Many people wrongly think that punishment is the best way to show their dog who's boss. In the past, a lot of dog training was overly corrective, using painful choke chains, for example, or the occasional smack. *Hurting a dog is always wrong.* It is also counterproductive. When you hit a dog, you teach him to fear you, you break his trust, and you weaken his confidence. Insecure dogs are the ones who are more likely to lash out in an aggressive display. It's understandable – you've given them nowhere else to go.

So how do you show the dog that you're a leader of his pack? Well, this is where an understanding of dog behavior really comes into its own.

Calm authority

As a leader you must show calm authority. Think of yourself as the managing director of your company. The dominant dog in a pack reveals his authority in his confident stance and aloofness. He's the boss and he knows it. You, too, must show your dog that you know best and you're in charge. Dogs pick up every nuance of human behavior. When we're upset, anxious, nervous, or stressed, our moods rub off on our four-legged friends. Projecting a calm, confident, and happy image will speak volumes to your dog.

Attention

Dogs, as social creatures, thrive on attention and are miserable when they are isolated. Dominant dogs get attention whenever they ask for it. To establish yourself as pack leader, don't respond every time your dog asks for your attention. Initiate contact with him on your terms. In the same way, ignoring your dog can help to calm him down if he is overly boisterous when he greets you. Wait until he has settled himself and then give him attention.

Keep on top

Dogs seeking attention or control often try to gain advantage by occupying valuable raised spaces such as a chair, sofa, or bed, for example. If your dog begins to guard these spaces from you, deny him access or only allow him to join you on these elevated areas when he is specifically invited by you. He should get "off" when you ask him to.

Food

In the wild, the pack leader enjoys the first taste of the kill and is able to choose the most tasty and nourishing portions of it. In the same way, the most dominant puppy in a litter will attach himself to the front teats of his mother, the ones that produce more milk and more protective antibodies. That means he will grow faster and bigger than the other pups, and will stay healthy and resist infections better in later life. To show your dog you are his leader, pretend to eat from his bowl before you feed him. If you are sitting down to supper at the same time as your dog is usually fed, make sure you feed him second. Never give him food from your plate.

If a dog has stolen food, however, do not challenge him to give it back, unless it poses a hazard to him. Accept that it belongs to him now. In the wild, if a lesser dog manages to take food from a more dominant individual, he will rarely be challenged. (See also Scavenging and stealing, page 107.)

Toys

As the leader, you should be in control of all the dog's toys. Make him sit before you give him a toy or play a game with him.

Territory

Dominant dogs decide where they sleep or rest, and have access to every part of their territory. To establish yourself as a leader, you must make it clear where your dog is allowed to go and where he is not allowed to go. Even if you let him onto your sofa, move him off occasionally and sit yourself in his place.

The senses

Much of the information the dog learns about the world, he receives through his senses. As human beings, our dominant sense is sight. We live in an intensely visual world. The same is not true of dogs. The richness of experience that we gain through our eyes is gained by the dog chiefly through his spectacular sense of smell.

The only time I came close to understanding what it was like to have a heightened sense of smell was when I was pregnant. For the first few months, a whole new world opened up to me. Even in my delicate state, I could still appreciate how incredible it was that I seemed to be able to smell *everything*. Of course, there was a downside to that. For a while I went around wearing a face mask in the hope that a certain smell wouldn't make me run for the bathroom, but unfortunately I could still smell sausages being cooked in the next city. And that is just a fraction of a dog's capacity. The dog has *forty* times more scent receptors in his nasal cavities than we do. The part of the dog's brain that processes scent information is also much more highly developed than our own. And you expect your dog not to want to be close to you when you're cooking and eating dinner?

Try putting your favorite food on the kitchen counter. Don't eat for five hours and then walk past without taking a bite. We expect our dogs to have amazing impulse control when we humans often have very little.

The dog has *forty* times more scent receptors in his nasal cavities than we do.

Smell

In the wild, the dog's highly developed sense of smell gives the species a great advantage when tracking down prey and identifying fellow pack members. Where we would size up a new situation with our eyes, dogs explore new environments by sniffing them. When they greet or meet other dogs, they will sniff them in what – to our eyes – are the most embarrassing places, places where odor is most concentrated.

Scent passes on an incredible amount of information to a dog. Scent-marking with urine or by leaving deposits from the sweat glands between the toes is the way dogs communicate and establish their territory. Sacs inside the dog's rectum also produce a scent that coats the feces. When you're out walking in the park with your dog, he's using his nose to pick up who's been there before him – perhaps a dominant dog, a female in heat, an old dog, a sick dog, or a dog he's already met. Dogs can smell females in heat who are miles away.

Sight

Dogs see very differently than human beings. Our field of vision is about 100 degrees. If we want to see things to the side, we have to turn our heads; if we want to see things behind, we have to turn around. Dogs have a much wider field of vision, which enables them to see to the sides and the rear. In sight hounds, such as Whippets and Greyhounds, the field of vision may be as much as double our own. While the positioning of the eyes in certain breeds may lessen that field of vision to some degree, all dogs have better peripheral vision than humans.

Contrary to popular belief, dogs aren't color-blind, but they don't see colors as well as we do, and find it difficult to tell the difference between certain shades such as red and green. In lower light conditions, they see much better than we do, thanks to a reflective layer at the back of their eyes called the tapetum lucidum. In the wild, this enables the dog to hunt at dawn and dusk, when their natural prey is more likely to be out and about.

What dogs are best at seeing, however, is movement. A dog can detect the slightest movement, which also has obvious advantages when it comes to tracking prey. The dog's extreme sensitivity to movement means that hand signals and gestures are often much more useful in training than spoken commands, especially if you are working at a distance. Close up, dogs don't see quite so well, and find it difficult to distinguish an object from its surroundings. If you put a treat on the floor right in front of your dog, he might find it hard to see – he'll rely on his nose to sniff it out.

Hearing

A dog's hearing is incredibly acute. Because dogs' ears are large and movable, they can detect where sounds are coming from more accurately than humans. They can also hear sounds over greater distances than we can – nearly five times as far – and they can hear sounds of a higher frequency that are inaudible to us: hence the dog whistle that is silent to human ears. Dogs communicate through many different vocalizations, from barking to whining.

Taste

Dogs are omnivores and will eat almost anything – including what we would not consider to be food! We may not think that dogs have a very sophisticated palate, but they do appreciate variety and get bored when all they encounter are the same tastes and textures. You can make training more pleasurable for your dog by offering food rewards that stimulate his taste buds. Meat treats are always popular, but cheese can also be very effective.

Touch

Dogs can't pick up and handle new objects to investigate them. Instead, much like human babies, they put them in their mouths. Mouthing is an important part of exploration for a dog, particularly for puppies. Special sensory hairs grow around the dog's muzzle, under his jaw, and above his eyes. These are called vibrissae, or more commonly, whiskers, and they also help him gather information about his environment through touch.

Human beings express their affection through touch, but this is not necessarily a natural response for a dog. Dogs have to become accustomed to gentle handling and stroking from puppyhood onward.

Play-biting in puppies is an important way that dogs learn how strong their bite is. If a puppy is separated too early from its littermates, as is often the case with pet store puppies, it may not have had the chance to learn what is called an "inhibited bite" and may be more prone to nipping.

Know yourself

Bringing a new puppy or dog into your home should never be an act of impulse. Before you make that decision, you need to ask yourself some searching questions. Dogs, as the slogan goes, are not just for Christmas, they're for life.

Just as it's difficult to appreciate before the event how much things will change when you have a baby, bringing a puppy into your life is a significant undertaking. When I got my first puppy, I was living in a fourth-floor apartment with no elevator in the heart of Manhattan. As a trainer, I knew what to expect, but even so it was quite an effort to go up and down those stairs twice a night so the puppy could have a pee. Nor was it particularly pleasant to walk him after dark on 46th Street!

If you have had dogs before, or if you had a dog when you were growing up, you may already have some idea of what's involved. If you have never owned a dog, think about the following issues:

Will you be able to spend enough time with your dog?
Once they are past the puppy stage, most dogs can be left for between four and six hours without becoming distressed. If you work full-time and there is no one else at home to look after the dog, you are condemning an essentially social creature to a life of anxiety, boredom, and depression, unless you hire a dog-sitter or enroll your dog at a doggy day-care center.

Dogs need regular exercise
That means a couple of walks and a decent run every day. Cats exercise themselves. Dogs, however, should not be left to stray without human supervision.

Dogs need training
Even the most seemingly docile animal can become a monster without basic obedience training. You need time to do this, and plenty of patience.

Dogs need stimulation
Just like us, they get bored without challenges, fun, and games.

Do you have children?
Have you got a dog already, or another pet? Settling a new canine arrival within a family can sometimes be difficult, especially if not everyone in your household is as overjoyed as you are at the prospect.

Which breed to choose?

Once you have satisfied yourself that you are prepared to meet the challenges that a dog will bring into your life, the next question is, which dog? Humans have been selectively breeding dogs for centuries, accentuating certain innate characteristics or aspects of appearance. While all dogs are individuals, each breed tends to have certain traits in common. Some need more exercise than others; some require more grooming. Some breeds are naturally more protective; others are more sensitive to noise.

The great advantage of choosing a purebred dog is that you will know to a certain extent what to expect. Use this to your advantage and do your research thoroughly beforehand. Read books and magazines, talk to breeders, and ask friends about their experiences with their dogs. Don't choose a dog on the basis of its appearance or because the breed is in fashion. Many people who rushed out to get a cute little Dalmatian after seeing 101 black-and-white spotted puppies cavorting in a Disney film found themselves owning a dog with substantial needs for exercise. Dalmatians were originally bred as "carriage dogs"; that is to say, they were bred to run alongside carriages and scare off footpads and thieves. They need exercise – tons of it – and careful, confident handling.

Choosing the right breed is choosing the breed that is right for your situation. If you want a laid-back, easygoing pet that will be a good companion for your children, a Terrier, which is a particularly active sort of dog, wouldn't be the most sensible choice. Labradors and Retrievers, on the other hand, are naturally good-tempered and sociable, which makes them ideal for families with children. However, they do need a lot of exercise. If you are not prepared to devote considerable time to training and exercising, don't choose a working dog such as a Border Collie, who will go crazy without sufficient stimulation. Greyhounds and Whippets, although bred to be very fast, paradoxically don't require vast amounts of exercise. The guarding breeds, such as German Shepherds, Rottweilers, Dobermans, Chows, and Akitas, are intelligent and loyal, but they can be over-protective and tend to be one-person dogs. It is important to know that while taking breed characteristics into account, every dog within that breed is an individual with his own unique personality and temperament.

Aspects to consider:

 Size
How big will the dog grow? And how much will he eat?

 Noise
Some breeds are naturally more inclined to bark and yap than others. Some breeds are more sensitive to noise.

 Activity level
How much exercise does the dog require? Working breeds, bred to herd sheep, need serious workouts.

 Temperament
Terriers are naturally bossy and tenacious. Spaniels, Setters, and Retrievers generally have friendly, affectionate natures.

 Coat
How much time (or money) will you need to devote to grooming?

 Weaknesses
Because of inbreeding, some breeds suffer from congenital problems. Dalmatians, for example, have a tendency to go deaf. British bulldogs can suffer from breathing problems. Cavalier King Charles Spaniels can have heart ailments.

Mongrels

Unlike acquiring a purebred dog, taking on a mongrel is necessarily more of a leap in the dark. Mongrels or crosses (dogs bred from two purebred parents) will have characteristics of different breeds in their makeup, and you may not be able to tell which characteristic will come to the fore. It may even be hard to gauge how large the dog will grow. The size of a puppy's feet may give some indication of how big he will get, but that is not an infallible guide.

On the plus side, many mongrels are good all-rounders. Many are particularly long-lived and, because they have a mixed gene pool, they are much less likely to suffer the congenital problems that result from inbreeding.

Where to find a puppy

Always acquire puppies from good, reputable sources. In the case of purebred animals, that means going direct to a breeder. No self-respecting dog-breeder would ever sell a litter to a pet store. My grandmother knew each of the Beagles she bred by name, and she took the trouble to visit them in their new homes.

You can find a reputable breeder by seeking advice from a national organization, such as the Kennel Club, or by contacting a breed's organization. Alternatively, you could ask for a recommendation from friends. You will know you have found a good breeder when he or she asks you more questions than you ask them. A good breeder will only sell a puppy to someone they think will treat him properly and give him the care that he needs. They'll want to know if you will be home during the day, if you have a garden, if there's a park nearby where you can exercise the dog. They'll give you advice on training and diet. They may want to come and see you at home.
Only when they're satisfied that you will make a good dog-owner will they sell you the puppy.

Mongrels and crossbred puppies, which are less sought after than purebreds, are less commonly found in pet stores, but it is just as inadvisable to acquire a mongrel in this way as it is a purebred pup. While the puppy may look cute and appealing, buying him from a pet store may leave you with an animal that has health problems or with one that has been affected by poor handling. Instead, look at advertisements in reputable magazines, or at the vet's, and visit the puppy at home before you decide to take him home.

Contrary to what pet shop proprietors may tell you, puppies in pet stores are more likely to come from puppy mills or farms. While there have been efforts to control this despicable practice, it still carries on.

Rescue dogs

An alternative source for both puppies and adult dogs is to visit a dogs' home, shelter, or rescue agency, and adopt a dog that has been abandoned. Rescue dogs have poor reputations, and many people consider that they are too unpredictable or too scarred by past ill treatment to be successfully re-homed. That is far from the case. Dogs end up in shelters for a wide variety of reasons. An unwanted litter may see the puppies abandoned; older dogs may be taken in if their owners are too elderly or sick to care for them. Greyhounds that have been raced professionally may be taken in by rescue agencies to prevent them from being put down when their racing days are over. Naturally enough, puppies are generally re-homed very quickly, while the older and more difficult dogs can take considerably longer to place. If you are considering giving a home to one of these unfortunate creatures, consult the shelter staff and be guided by their appraisal of each dog's characteristics and what it needs in the form of support.

A large proportion of dogs that are in shelters are there due to behavior problems; that is, behaviors that are natural for the dog but unacceptable in our society. It is easier to blame problem behavior on a dog's character than to look at how the environment we have created might be affecting it. Most of these problem behaviors can be modified with a little time and understanding.

Many people consider rescue dogs too unpredictable or too scarred by past ill-treatment to be successfully re-homed—that is far from the case.

Here's an all-too-common scenario:

Lily is a typical puppy who, like a human baby, needs constant stimulation and guidance from her human pack for healthy development. Instead, she finds herself in a home where this support is lacking, and in an environment that is physically and mentally isolating. In order to cope with her insecurity, Lily begins to demonstrate increasingly desperate, attention-seeking behavior, which changes this picture-book puppy into an unwanted presence and a time-consuming menace.

Struggling to understand her human world, Lily has no idea that she is living on borrowed time, until she finds herself at the doors of the local shelter. She enters a bizarre world where she experiences high levels of stress in response to the new sights, sounds, and smells surrounding her.

The routine changes. She is fed strange food, which she doesn't feel like eating. Her new home is cramped and smells of disinfectant. She senses tension emanating from the dogs around her, and endures a constant stream of strange faces passing by her pen. In order to cope with these pressures, Lily hides under a security blanket of self-preservation, her true behavior numbed by this alien environment.

However, fortune favors her when she is adopted by a new human pack. She responds well to their attention and they, in turn, are pleased with her response. Her world changes again, but this time the environment is calmer. The bed smells good and the food is tasty. The pressures of shelter life begin to fall away.

For the first weeks, the numbness that protected Lily at the shelter keeps her from showing her true colors, but renewed confidence awakens previous patterns of behavior that soon challenge her new owners. Their attempts at control cause confusion and turmoil. Unable to cope with their "problem," the new owners take Lily back to the shelter. This time she is not so lucky. Her unpredictability is deemed a liability for prospective adopters, and her life is ended by the vet's needle.

This is not a sob story. This is the reality for millions of dogs each year. According to the Humane Society of America, between six and ten million dogs are put down in American shelters every year, and only 5% of these for medical reasons. In Britain, a nation of dog-lovers, the figures are a vast improvement, but there is no cause for complacency. Around 20,000 unwanted and stray dogs are put down each year, and that's still 20,000 too many.

What can we do to help adopted shelter dogs adapt to their new lives? First and foremost, rescue dogs take time and patience. The type of training outlined in subsequent chapters of this book can be used to address certain types of problem behavior that shelter dogs may display. Equally important, it is necessary to understand why dogs behave the way that they do, to see the world from their point of view. This is always important, but it is even more critical when a dog has been ill-treated or abandoned.

The effort is worth it. With renewed confidence, the shelter dog can develop into what he was always meant to be: a happy and healthy companion that deserves our time and respect for coping with all the pressures that human life has thrown at him.

It is easier to blame problem behavior on a dog's character than to look at how the environment we have created might be affecting it.

Should I have my dog neutered?

The short answer is "yes." Having a dog spayed (removing the ovaries and uterus) or neutered (removing the testicles) is an important part of responsible dog ownership. Your dog will be healthier, more contented, could live longer, and will behave better without his sexual urges confusing the picture. Many people are reluctant to have their pets neutered because it seems unnatural. But if you do not intend to breed your dog, what is more unnatural, allowing him to suffer the insistent tugs of instincts he cannot fulfill, or removing the urge completely?

Neutering our dogs is the most significant way we can reduce the huge problem caused by unwanted dogs. Millions are taken into shelters every year. Perhaps you imagine that letting your dog have just one litter wouldn't make much of a difference. Think again. If you placed all the puppies from that litter in the homes of people who thought the same, and they did likewise, your dog could be responsible for the birth of 200 puppies in a single year.

Neutering our dogs is the most significant way we can reduce the huge problem caused by unwanted dogs.

Effects on temperament

Neutering has only positive effects on a dog's temperament. Dogs of either sex will be calmer and better behaved.

An un-neutered male dog is more likely to stray. If he can smell a female in heat – she doesn't have to be next door, she might be a mile away – he will try his utmost to get to her. Dogs have been known to throw themselves at glass doors. Once he's out, he might be hit by a car, attacked by another dog, or picked up and put in a shelter. Entire dogs (those who have not been neutered) are less easygoing at home. They are more likely to scent-mark with urine. They are prone to mounting furniture and people. And they may be more aggressive. Neutered dogs, on the other hand, focus on their owners.

Female dogs in heat attract males from far and wide. An un-neutered female will have about two seasons a year, each period lasting about three weeks. There will be a bloody discharge for the first week, but the dog will remain fertile for two further weeks. Females sometimes mark their territory, too. They may be more aggressive, restless, and irritable.

Effects on health

A spayed or neutered animal could live a longer, healthier life than an entire dog. Neutered dogs tend to live an average of two to three years longer than un-neutered dogs.

Spaying a female or neutering a male are veterinary procedures performed under general anesthesia. The dog will require just an overnight stay and should be back to normal a couple of days later.

Neutering a young male dog helps to prevent testicular cancer, prostate disease, and hernias. Spaying a female dog helps prevent uterine infections and mammary cancer, and spaying before the first heat offers the best protection from these diseases. Contrary to popular belief, females should not be allowed to have a litter before they are spayed. Neither does neutering mean that your dog will gain weight. If he does, you're feeding him too much or not exercising him enough.

Talk Dog communicating with your dog

Let me begin by stating the obvious: Dogs do not speak English. Or French, or German, or Spanish, for that matter. They talk dog.

The secret of successful training is to learn how to communicate with your dog in a way that he understands. He can't learn your language. It's up to you to learn to speak his.

Dogs are terrific communicators. Have you ever stopped to think how many different words we have for the noises dogs make – words such as growl, snarl, whine, whimper, bark, and howl? All these various sounds and vocalizations mean different things in dog language, while the meanings may also change in subtle ways, depending on context and circumstance.

Then there's body language. Dogs communicate with sound, but they also speak volumes through their gestures and stances. A lift of an eyebrow, a yawn, a wrinkled brow are just some of the ways they signal their feelings and intentions to others, both canine and human.

Learning to talk dog is the key to understanding your pet so that you can better meet his needs. This chapter covers the range of sounds and signals that form the basis of canine communication. With a little practice, you'll be speaking it like a native!

The secret of successful
training is to learn how
to communicate with
your dog in a way that
he understands.

Sounds and vocalizations

Dogs bark. It's what they do. But they make a wide range of other sounds, too, and here is what they each mean:

Whining

The very first form of vocalization is the whine. Puppies whine to gain the attention of their mother. In adult dogs, this insistent, rather nagging, high-pitched sound is similarly often a request for you to take some notice. "Feed me!" it says. "Let me out!" Or simply, "Pay me some attention!" Whining can also indicate that the dog is nervous, frightened, or anxious.

Whimpering

When whining shades into the more pitiful sound of whimpering, it can be the sign of more serious distress – dogs often whimper when they are in pain. Otherwise, it could simply be the dog's way of intensifying or heightening the plea of whining, particularly when it is accompanied by pawing. "What would it take to get you to pay some attention to me?" it says.

Yelping

A sudden yelp is a pain cry. If you accidentally step on a dog's paw or tail, he'll yelp to let you know that he's hurt.

Growling

The growl is the dog's key warning sound. But it is also an important part of the way puppies play. Play-fighting is how puppies test the waters, see how far they can go and how strong they are, and growling often goes along with it. When older dogs play with each other, they revert to this puppyish behavior and may growl at each other without intending to communicate aggression. When your dog plays with you – for example, when you're playing tugging games – he may also emit a wavering growl. It doesn't mean he's going to snap at you, it's just part of the mock battle you're playing.

When a growl is deep and sustained, and is accompanied by a tense body, it's a clear warning to back off. This is the sign of impending aggression. The dog may feel threatened or under attack, and is giving you or another dog the chance to avoid further trouble before it's too late.

Snarling

"You didn't listen, did you?" When the warning given by the growl goes unheeded, the vocalization escalates. The growl goes up a level in intensity and vibrates a little, becoming less sustained. The lips are up and the teeth are bared. Snarling indicates that aggressive action is imminent.

Howling

Many people interpret the long mournful tone of the howl as a sound of distress. While it's true that dogs will often howl if left alone too long – "Where are you, my human pack?" – howling doesn't necessarily indicate unhappiness. The howl is the biggest sound a dog can make, and it carries over long distances. In the wild, it is used to signal a dog's presence to others or to ward off predators. Some dogs – notably basset hounds – are more prone to howling than others. Dogs will also howl in response to the bark or howl of another dog. And, of course, we all know that some dogs like to howl along to the piano, no matter how well you are playing!

Champing

You may never have heard the term before, but if you're a dog owner, you'll probably recognize champing when you hear it. It's a type of sucking, chewing noise that a dog makes – as if he were a horse champing at a bit, or as if he were licking his chops, except that he will make this noise when he is not actually eating. This is a pacifying sound. Some dogs "champ" when they are greeting humans or other canines; others do it to show that they are not a threat.

Groaning

Many dogs make a low, throaty, murmuring groan, moan, or growl when they are being stroked. This indicates bliss and pleasure.

Barking

Barking is a really important part of dog communication. Depending on the context, it has a variety of meanings. Barking can be used to sound an alarm or warning, it can be a call for attention, or it may simply indicate that the dog is excited. Dogs bark to signal their presence to other dogs that may not be able to see them – that bad dog on the other side of the fence, for example. They also bark in response to barking or to mark their territory. And, of course, they bark when they are bored and isolated. While excessive barking may indicate a problem, it is very important that dogs should be able to bark from time to time. It's wrong to expect a dog to spend his life in silence.

When they are very young, puppies do not bark. Timing varies, but in most cases a puppy will have started to bark by the age of two months. Some breeds also bark more than others. Maltese dogs are pretty vocal, and so are Shelties. Dachshunds are also predisposed to bark, for good reason. They were originally bred to go down holes after badgers and to bark when they found them so that hunters could identify exactly where the badgers were (the breed name means "badger dog" in German).

Body language

Body language is vital in dog communication. Take the time
to observe your dog closely in different situations, and try to work
out what he is trying to say by watching his body language.

Signals pass between dogs faster than we can see – literally in
the blink of an eye. Owners often call me to say that they were just
walking their dog along the road when another dog coming toward
them lunged out aggressively with no warning, and without their dog
doing anything at all. Or vice versa – sometimes it was the owner's
dog that instigated the aggression. It may seem that nothing has
provoked the behavior, but in that split second, those two dogs
have been signaling to each other and have sized each other up.
We humans are often very unobservant. Dogs, on the other hand,
don't miss a trick. Even a small lift of the eyebrow speaks volumes.

Humans rely heavily on verbal communication. But we send out
many physical signals of our own. In drama workshops, students are
often asked to stand in front of another person in the group and try
to communicate with them using only facial expressions. A great
actor can show you what he or she is feeling without uttering a
word. You can try it yourself at home with a friend.

What follows is a description of what your dog is saying with his
body language. Each part of the body acts in conjunction with other
parts, so you can't simply read the signs in isolation. Reading the
body signals as a whole will tell you what your dog is feeling.

**In the dog, facial expressions
in particular can be very subtle,
which is why we humans often
miss and misread them. It does
not help matters that breeding for
appearance has greatly affected
the ability of dogs to communicate
effectively with each other and
with us. Flattened noses, overly
wrinkled skin, and docked tails are
just some of the ways in which our
strange notions of canine
"beauty" have compromised the
dog's means of expressing himself.**

Ears

Let's start at the top. It's easiest to distinguish ear signals on dogs with pointed ears. Dogs with drooping ears, such as Beagles and Spaniels, use their ears to signal in the same way, but the signs are slightly harder to see.

Ears that stick straight up represent alertness, confidence, and awareness. If the ears are drawn back on the head, your dog is showing friendliness, that is provided vigorous tail-wagging, a wriggling body, and a calm, relaxed facial expression accompany it.

However, the ears can also be drawn back when the dog is nervous. In this case, the gesture is designed to be pacifying. It says: "I'm nervous, so please back off!" If so, there will be a number of other nervous signals. The tail may be between the legs, the body may be crouching, the front paw may be lifted, the eyes could be slightly closed with dilated pupils, or the mouth may be slightly open while the lips are licked.

Forehead

A wrinkled forehead suggests aggression. A smooth forehead, on the other hand, if it is accompanied by other relaxed body signals, indicates that the dog is relaxed. Or it may be a sign of submission if you notice other signals that indicate insecurity, such as a tail that is lowered or tucked between the dog's legs, a crouching stance, or a curved back.

Eyebrows

Roger Moore, the actor, makes wonderful use of the eyebrow lift. So does my husband. Just a slight lift of the eyebrow communicates that he's unhappy with something that I've said or done. It gets me every time. When a dog is trying to dominate a situation or assert control, the eyebrows seem almost to jump out at you as they are pushed forward, and the dog will stare at you in a challenging way. When a dog is calm, his eyebrows will not be pronounced.

Eyes

Stand in front of a friend or family member and ask that person to stare at you. Does it make you feel a little uncomfortable? At the very least, it will make you laugh. When a stranger stares at you, however, it's usually very disconcerting. Do you stare back, or do you break the stare and look away? If both of you keep staring at each other, the chances are that some sort of challenge is going on.

The stare means the same in dog talk. Staring at another dog or human is a sign of dominance, or may indicate an aggressive challenge. The eyes are wide and unflinching. If the stare is accompanied by other aggressive signs such as raised hackles, leaning forward, and stillness of the body, then you would do well to pay attention and stay away! However, a dog that is staring at you is not necessarily exhibiting aggression. It could just be that he is confident and attentive.

When a dog is insecure, he narrows his eyes and looks away from you to show that he poses no threat. Blinking is another important eye signal. Dogs often blink to show you they are friendly. Sometimes, however, they blink when they are frightened.

Mouth

The lips are often used to demonstrate aggression. One such signal, a slight lifting of the lips on one side, is incredibly subtle and may be hard to spot. When the lips are completely drawn forward, this indicates a more assertive form of aggression. When the lips are drawn back, this often signals an aggressive response that is the result of fear. Either way the teeth are exposed. A friend of mine owned a dog that would draw back her lips and expose her teeth when greeting you affectionately. Perhaps the dog simply didn't know what she was feeling, but I always swore she was smiling.

Lip smacking or licking with the tongue are signs of lack of confidence, stress, or fear, but are also used as pacifying gestures. Both wrinkle the muzzle, which is otherwise smooth when the dog is relaxed.

Neck

A confident dog will hold his neck straight and upright. A dog with less confidence will hold his neck lower. He may expose his throat to a dog that is more dominant. Exposing the throat says: "Hey, I'm no threat. I'm trusting you with a very delicate part of my body. And I'm turning my teeth away from you." If this submissive gesture is successful, then the more dominant dog will expose his throat, too, in order to show that he is accepting the submission and poses no threat, either.

Back

My grandmother stood with a straight back until the day she died. She had good posture, but she was a proud, confident woman and carried herself that way. The same goes for dogs: A straight back means confidence. A back that is curled means that the dog is insecure and submissive.

Hackles

When a dog is nervous or scared, this triggers a chain reaction of physiological responses that raises the hairs on the back of the neck and down the spine. The effect is to make the dog look bigger and fiercer. He's saying, "Don't mess with me. I'm bigger and stronger than you!"

Tail

The tail is important for both balance and signaling, which is why it is a huge shame that the practice of tail docking still continues. How would you feel if an important part of your body that you relied upon for expressing yourself were cut off? Without its tail, a dog is unable to communicate properly, which means that other dogs may miss vital signals.

The tail is a prime indicator of a dog's mood. A confident dog will hold his tail high in the air. It is possible that this allows scent from the anal glands to circulate more freely in the air and advertise his presence. A tail that is held low between the legs means that the dog is fearful and submissive.

Vigorous wagging usually means excitement, friendliness, and happiness. A tail that is held high but wagged more slowly means a cautious confidence. A tail that is held still and straight indicates a problem of some sort. One that is still, extended, and slightly curved says: "Get lost because I mean business!"

Paws

When my cat is feeling particularly affectionate, she will jump up and start kneading my leg with her paws. This is enjoyable for her because it's what she used to do to her mother in order to stimulate the teats into producing milk. Puppies do a similar thing, while adult dogs will paw at a person or another dog for attention and as a pacifying gesture. One of the reasons why it's usually easy to teach a dog to give his paw is that the gesture is already part of their vocabulary.

A paw placed over the neck of another dog, however, signals a challenge. Placing two paws around the neck tends to be a prelude either to a fight or to mating. Both genders, even when neutered, may mount other dogs, pieces of furniture, or, even more embarrassingly, your leg. Mounting or humping is not just a sexual behavior, it can also be a sign that a dog wants to control or dominate another dog or human.

In this context, it is easy to see why many dogs don't enjoy being hugged. We humans hug to show affection. But what is a hug to a dog but two very large paws placed over his neck? You're telling him you love him, but he might think you're being controlling.

The stomach

Most dogs love to have their tummies stroked and will flop onto their backs happily to invite you to do so. This clear body signal is a submissive gesture that your dog learned as a puppy. While play-fighting, puppies like to pin each other down, practicing the body signals they will need as adults. Showing the opponent the stomach puts the dog in a vulnerable position. It says: "I trust you enough to show you the most delicate part of me. I am no threat to you whatsoever."

But there is another side to this signal. After a kill, wild dogs and wolves always go for the stomach of the prey first. For good reason: Entrails contain the most nutrients. When a nervous dog lies on his back to show you his stomach, he is not inviting your touch, he is asking you to back off.

The play-bow

The play-bow is an invitation to play and a demonstration of friendliness. It's a very distinctive posture. The dog will lower his front quarters and bow down on his front legs, placing them flat on the ground in front of his body. His body will be curved, and the tail will be curved or wagging. The play-bow is often accompanied by a couple of short barks. It's a very engaging stance, and one a dog will sometimes adopt if he's been scolded.

Sniffing

Dogs do a lot of sniffing: It's their most important way of exploring the world around them. Sometimes, however, a dog will sniff the ground to calm another dog down and show him that he is not a threat. He's saying: "I'm much more interested in this patch of grass than you."

Yawning

This is an easy one, you might think. What else could yawning mean but tiredness? Well, that's not always the case. Yawning can mean a dog feels stressed and nervous. It can be used as a distraction or a calming signal. We humans do it, too, in situations that make us feel uncomfortable.

Scratching

Like yawning, scratching can also be a displacement activity. Humans bite their nails when they're anxious; dogs scratch. I often see a lot of scratching when I start to train a dog.

Sneezing

Similarly, sneezing can also be related to stress and anxiety. Insecure dogs often sneeze when meeting another dog or greeting a human.

Stretching

Dogs stretch for the same reason we do, to relieve muscle tension when moving from a sedentary pose to a more active one. But they may also stretch as a distraction or as a displacement activity in situations where they do not feel very comfortable.

Freezing

There are three principal ways in which a dog will respond to a threat: He'll run away, which is generally the most sensible option; he'll fight, if he feels up to it; or he'll freeze and hope that the threat goes away. If you touch a nervous dog and he freezes or his body tenses up, take your cue from that and back off. If you keep on stroking him, the next stage will be a warning growl, then a snarl, then a nip. Some dogs don't even bother to give a warning, but go straight to a bite.

Freezing is also a common stance when a dog spots something he perceives as prey. It may be a squirrel in the garden; it may be a bird. He'll stand stock-still, his entire attention focused on that creature.

Circling

When dogs circle on a spot, it indicates a range of different intentions and emotions. Typically, dogs circle just before settling themselves down to sleep or rest. In the wild, dogs choose sleeping places that are hidden in long grass, and circling serves to stamp down the grasses to form a comfortable bed. That same behavior survives in our domestic animals.

Circling is also an indication that the dog is getting ready to eliminate. He will circle a few times and then squat before defecating.

In some cases, circling can indicate anxiety or excitement. A dog that knows he is about to be fed, walked, or played with may twirl about on the floor as if he can barely contain himself. A slow circling, however, with a crouched posture and lowered head, indicates suspicion and unease.

Mixed signals

I have already discussed how hugging your dog can send him a mixed message. But there are other ways in which we fail to spot the signs or don't understand what a dog is trying to tell us.

When I was pregnant, strangers in the street would come up to me as if they knew me and, without asking if they could, would reach out and touch my stomach. It seemed that because I was a carrying a baby, this gave everyone carte blanche to touch me. Now they do the same to my baby.

It's very disconcerting when perfect strangers touch you for no reason at all or without your express invitation to do so. Yet we do the same thing to dogs all the time. Without asking, we go straight into their personal space, extend a big hand over their head, look them in the eye, and smile. We think we're being friendly. What a sensitive or nervous dog sees, however, is this:

"That stranger is coming up to me. He's getting close, too close! That big paw is coming over my head. What's he going to do? He's touching my head. I'm going to crouch down and see if he goes away. No good! I'm crouching and he hasn't gotten the message. He's touching me and staring and showing me his teeth. OK, I'm going to turn my head away. He's still touching me. Right. Now I'm going to turn my whole body away so that he'll know that I'm no threat to him and he can back off. He's still here. Now I'm really scared. I'll lift up my lip a little just to give him a warning that I'm uncomfortable. Warning not taken! OK, then how about a growl? Everyone understands what that means. Grrrrrrrr! Warning not taken. That's it, I've had enough. Now I have to protect myself the only way I know how. Ow! Why did my owner hit me? Couldn't he see that I was nervous and trying to get that man to back off, but he wouldn't listen until I tried to bite him?"

Nine times out of ten, the dog gets the blame for this sort of behavior. If you have a dog that is nervous around strangers and lunges aggressively when people come to greet him, chances are that he gave all of those passive calming signals the first couple of times that someone new came to greet him, but those signals were ignored. The only thing that worked was when he elevated his warning into a growl or into a lunge and then attempted to bite. Now every time he meets that same situation, it's straight to "go." He's not going to bother with all of the passive signals. He's going to go straight for what really works. From his point of view, it was only the attempted bite that was successful in making the stranger back off.

We all have a personal space surrounding us like a bubble. Some people are allowed into that space and others are not. Apart from those annoying people who like to get really close to someone while talking to them, completely ignoring the fact that they are trying to back away, most people respect personal space rules and won't invade that space uninvited. So why do we invade our dog's space all the time? This puts a tremendous amount of pressure on a nervous dog in particular, but we humans just don't understand, and will blame the dog if it reacts in a negative way.

Should you never greet a dog? Of course you can and should, but in a specific way. Instead of reaching that big hand over his head, bending down and staring into his eyes, keep upright, have your hand by your side, knuckles facing the dog, and just stand there. Say, "Hi," look at the dog briefly, then look away. Look again, then look away. Practice some dog talk by communicating those passive, nonthreatening signals. Allow the dog to make his own decisions about whether he wants to greet you or not. If he comes up to smell you, that's a promising sign. If not, then he has decided that he would rather not meet you today, and you should respect that.

I have a constant battle with people on the street who want to come up and greet dogs I'm working with. When I ask them not to, because the dog is a little nervous around strangers, they reply: "Oh it's fine, I'm great with dogs. Dogs love me." If they were truly understanding and good with dogs, they would appreciate why they had been asked to stay away, and would respect the wishes

of the owner or handler. Every dog is different and responds in
a different way.

I mentioned earlier that when a dog lies on his back and shows
you his stomach, it doesn't necessarily mean that he wants you to
play with him. If you do not know the dog or the dog is of a nervous
disposition and he lies on his back when you go to greet him, do not
continue the greeting. Stand up straight and back away slightly,
turning your head and averting your eyes. Respect that the dog has
given you a clear warning.

On one occasion I witnessed what happened when a man went
to greet a dog that was running around in a back garden. The man
was a stranger to the dog. The dog began to crouch and circle with
his tail tucked between his legs. As he got lower to the ground, he
bowed his head and flipped onto his back. The man, thinking that
the dog wanted to play with him, approached and began to stroke the
dog's stomach. The dog tensed, and before the man even knew what
had happened, the dog had bitten him and run away. The man was
upset because he was absolutely positive that the dog wanted to
have his stomach stroked and couldn't understand why he had been
bitten. He had completely misread the dog's signals and suffered a
deep bite to the hand as a consequence. This man had owned dogs
all his life.

Once a dog is comfortable with you or another family member,
he will allow you to break some of the rules. Then you can hug,
stroke, and cuddle him to your heart's content because he will
understand that you are no threat to him.

Allow the dog to make his own decisions
about whether he wants to greet you or not.

Dog School basic obedience training

A confident dog is relaxed,
alert, happy, and secure.

Training your dog is essential. It establishes lines of communication so that you and your dog can understand each other. It builds a strong bond between you and your pet. And it gives your dog confidence.

Many people mistake bossiness and assertiveness in a dog for confidence. Confidence is very different. A confident dog is relaxed, alert, happy, and secure. He's not trying to control you or the environment he finds himself living in. Instead, he knows that he can rely on you to protect him and meet his needs – not merely his physical need to be fed and exercised, but also his very real need for stimulation, affection, and play.

Training is not about imposing types of behavior on your dog that are alien to his nature. It's not about making your dog fearful or breaking his will. It's giving him the tools to live in your world. You wouldn't bring a puppy into your home and not house-train him. Training a dog to come when you call him or to stay when you tell him to is just as important. A trained dog is not only better behaved, he's safer.

Dogs are eager to learn. Their brains need stimulation, just like ours. Spending the time to educate and train your dog will set him up for life. It takes time and patience, but it doesn't have to be a chore. Training should be a positive, ongoing experience, an opportunity for you and your dog to have fun.

How dogs learn

Before you enroll your dog in a training class, employ a private trainer, or begin to train your dog yourself, you need to understand how dogs learn, because, like humans, dogs learn about the world in a variety of ways.

Instinct

Some of the dog's knowledge is preprogrammed. As soon as a puppy is born, he moves toward his mother's teat in order to feed. No one has taught the puppy to do this. He knows instinctively that he must eat to survive. The hunting instinct is very strong in adult dogs. Although your dog does not have to hunt for the food that you give him, that instinct is what kept his ancestors alive and ensured the survival of the species.

Breeding

Selective breeding has added another complexion to your dog's makeup. Retrievers retrieve, Pointers point, Terriers dig. Humans have accentuated some aspects of natural dog behavior through breeding to make working dogs more useful to them. If your dog is a Maltese, you have to accept that you might never train him to retrieve. It's just not in his nature. Every dog is an individual, but if you own a purebred animal, be aware of common traits and characteristics.

Like humans, dogs learn that there are consequences to their behavior.

Environment and experience

The dog comes equipped with certain traits and instincts. However, much of what he learns about the world, he picks up from his environment. Babies learn by watching their parents and siblings and copy what they do. It's the same with puppies. As soon as they are born, puppies are busy gathering information about the world through their littermates, their mother, and the humans who care for them. And they mimic the behavior of their littermates and other dogs.

If a puppy is removed from his mother and littermates too early, he misses out on an important learning stage. All that rough and tumble is not simply exuberance or high spirits. When puppies play-fight, they are learning how to read signals, how to inhibit their bite, and how to get along with each other.

As soon as we bring that puppy home, it is our responsibility to ensure that he experiences good things and lives in an environment that promotes positive learning. We need to manage the environment on the dog's behalf, socializing him so that he does not fear other people, exposing him in a careful and controlled way to a variety of experiences that will stimulate his senses and his brain.

Conditioning

One of the most important ways dogs learn is by conditioning. There are two main ways in which this works.

If I reach into a box and pull out a delicious piece of chocolate cake, chances are that I am going to do it again, because the result of my action was so pleasurable. Like humans, dogs learn that there are consequences to their behavior. If the consequences are pleasant, the dog will be inclined to repeat the action, and vice versa. Say, for example, but he gets a treat when he sits. He'll be more likely to sit the next time you ask him because of the reward. Suppose you ask him to sit, but he doesn't obey the signal, and therefore doesn't get the reward. Then you ask him to sit again, he sits, and he gets the reward this time. Sooner or later, he's going to work out that sitting when he's asked to sit is much more pleasurable than not sitting when he's asked. This type of conditioning is called "operant" conditioning.

The second type of conditioning, known as "classic" conditioning, has to do with making associations. In the late 1970s, when I was a child, there was an ad on TV for a certain sweet that was supposed to make your mouth water. A catchy little jingle accompanied the campaign. Every time I went into a shop to buy that particular sweet, my mouth would start watering. It still happens to me 30 years later. Thanks to the ad campaign, my brain associates the sight of those sweets with mouth watering.

Dogs make these kinds of associations all the time. The rattle of the leash means he's going to get walked. The ring of the doorbell means that someone is going to come in through the door. The sight of the vet's coat means the possibility of pain.

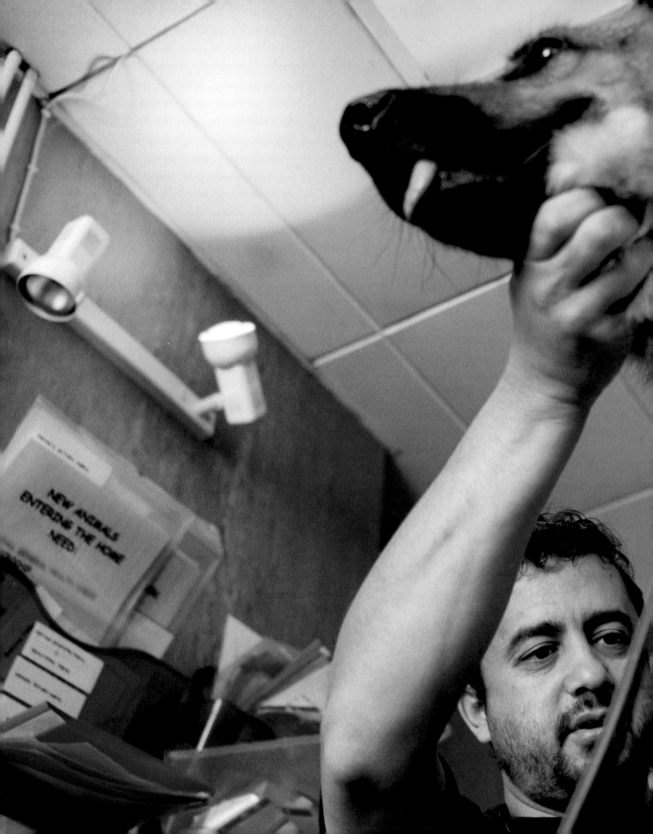

The power of positive training

Now that you understand how a dog learns, you can start teaching him the things that he needs to know. All my training techniques are positive, and yours should be, too. I use rewards to back up good behavior and to reinforce learning. I use vocal corrections to alert the dog to the fact that he has not behaved in the way he is supposed to. I never use harsh punishment.

Shouting, screaming, yelling, hitting, and smacking are absolute no-nos. They have no place in dog training. If you lash out at a dog, verbally or physically, you teach him fear and disrespect. He won't trust you. Instead, he will associate you with bad feelings. You will become the source of nasty experiences.

You don't need fancy equipment to train a dog. You need time and patience – and a sense of fun! All dog training is based on a combination of vocal commands and physical signals. Both are required to train a dog effectively. Dogs watch us more closely than they listen to us. They find it difficult to understand words. In some circumstances, when they're halfway across the park, for example, they may not hear us very clearly. But they will be able to see a hand signal and understand what it means.

Shouting, screaming, yelling, hitting, and smacking are absolute no-nos. They have no place in dog training.

Timing

What's the secret of comedy? Timing. Without it, the comedian "dies" on stage. Communicating with your dog effectively relies on perfect timing. Because you both speak the same language, you can explain to a child why a past action was wrong. Dogs do not have these language skills. They will only associate a behavior with a reward, or a behavior with a correction, if the time between the two is very short. We're talking about one second! You must deliver your feedback within one second of the behavior. For example, if you don't reward the dog for sitting as soon as he has put his bottom on the floor, you may well be rewarding a head turn rather than the behavior you wanted to reward, which was the dog putting his bottom on the floor. It is as defined as that. This doesn't mean you have to shove food into his mouth or give him a toy within a second of him sitting. Just come in quickly with "good dog" before you give any other reward. You can't punish a dog for peeing on the floor if you did not see him do it. Neither can you punish him for chewing the cushion if you didn't catch him in the act.

Split-second timing is important for another reason. You are teaching the dog to take action immediately and not to hesitate when a command is given. This will help him respond to you more quickly when you need to use a command at a time of real distraction or heightened emotion.

Consistency

Consistency is very important when it comes to teaching your dog to function in this strange domestic world that they have to live in. Dogs see things in black and white, while we humans have a lot of gray areas. Can the dog sit on the couch or not? If one of you allows the dog on the couch and the other tells the dog off each time it jumps up there, what message are you sending? Mixed messages confuse dogs and continual confusion makes them anxious.

Consistency is also essential in training. Everyone in the household should use the same commands and gestures, just as they should agree on the same rules – and that includes dog-walkers, sitters, and anyone else who is looking after your dog on a regular basis. Inconsistency is one of the most common problems I see when I'm advising clients.

Using your voice

People are always telling me that they know that their dog understands them when they talk to them. Dogs are very perceptive animals, and of course they understand some of what their owners say. But they don't understand the words because they speak our language. They know what's being said because they associate certain sounds with certain outcomes. When you train a dog to perform a specific activity, you link the sound of a word to a particular behavior and reinforce the association with praise and a treat. Once the dog has learned the command, the sound of "sit" will be linked in the dog's mind to the fact he has to put his rear end on the ground. And then when he does, something good happens. It's not that the dog understands what "sit" means. You could link that simple act of sitting to any word – "fly," for example – if you started by teaching that word. This is why we can confuse our dogs when we have taught them what "sit" means but then ask them to "sit down" or "sit sit sit." "What in the world does "sit sit sit" mean?" thinks the dog.

Tone and pitch

Have you ever heard of the term "motherese"? This is the way we often speak to our babies and our pets. Our voice is pitched very high and we speak in a baby-like way. Babies and dogs love it. It is a nonthreatening, calming, and safe way of communicating. When we get angry or administer a correction, our tone of voice becomes deeper and more threatening. Our dogs respond really well to vocal tone and pitch.

Keep your commands or vocal cues short and simple, two words at most.

Using hand signals

Vocal cues can be paired with physical signals, as well as being used on their own. I think dogs pick up what we are trying to teach them quicker that way. It's harder for humans to be consistent with their gestures than it is for them to be consistent with words. Decide which signal you are going to use for a particular command, and stick with it. Your hands must say the same thing as your mouth. If you point to a dog when you tell him to sit, and also make the same gesture when you ask him to stay, how is he supposed to know what to do?

Keep your gestures subtle and contained. You don't have to wave your arms around.

Common cues and signals

I don't really like the word "command." We are not commanding our dogs from on high, we are giving them cues and signals to show them how we want them to behave. The following are the words and signals that I like to use. You can use any words or signals you like, as long as you are consistent.

COME
Meaning: Come back to me from a distance.
Signal: I pat my chest or my legs, and I turn my body in the direction I want the dog to come.

SIT
Meaning: Put your bottom on the floor.
Signal: I hold my hand in front of the dog's nose, as if I was going to give him a treat. Then I raise my wrist slightly.

DOWN
Meaning: Lie down on your belly.
Signal: I start by placing the flat of my hand on the ground. As training goes on, I lower my hand but don't put it right on the ground.

UP
Meaning: Get up from a down position to a sitting one.
Signal: I clap my hands and say "up-up-up" in a high, motivated tone.

STAND
Meaning: Get up from a sitting position to stand on all four legs.
Signal: I raise my arm from the elbow with my palm facing upward.

STAY
Meaning: Do not move until I give you the release command.
Signal: I stretch out my hand in front of me, palm facing outward toward the dog.

OKAY
Meaning: You may move now.
No hand signal. Just an energetic vocal signal and body movement to motivate the dog.

OFF
Meaning: Take your paws off the sofa, kitchen counter, bed, and so on.
Signal: I point to where I want the dog to go and move my eyes toward the place where I am pointing.

WATCH ME
Meaning: Focus on my face. Give me eye contact. I want your attention.
Signal: I raise my hand up to my eyes.

HEEL
Meaning: Walk by my left or right heel or thigh. Stop when I stop. Walk when I walk.
Signal: I slap my left thigh (or my right), depending on whether I feel more comfortable walking the dog on my left or my right.

STOP (used when walking the dog)
Meaning: Stop right next to me.
Signal: I put my hand down by my side, palm facing the dog.

LET'S GO
Meaning: Walk with me. You can walk slightly in front of me or at the side, but do not pull me.
No hand signal. Just an energetic vocal and body signal.

LEAVE IT

Meaning: **Take your nose away from an object, person, dog, or piece of food.**

No hand signal.

DROP IT

Meaning: **Release an object from your mouth.**

No hand signal.

TAKE IT

Meaning: **Take an object into your mouth.**

No hand signal.

GENTLE

Meaning: **Take a treat from my hand in a gentle manner. Do not grab.**

No hand signal.

Giving your dog
a reward when he
does what you ask
will motivate him
to do it again.

Rewards

What is going to motivate a dog to learn? A reward. Giving your dog a reward when he does what you ask will motivate him to do it again. We all need motivation. What would happen if your employer didn't pay you? You would certainly be less keen to go to work.

Think about what motivates your dog the most. Food treats work well with most dogs. Other good rewards are toys such as squeakies, tug ropes, and tennis balls, as well as petting, praise, exercise, and play. Vary the motivators that you use in training so they don't become boring. If your dog doesn't know what reward he will be getting next, it keeps him interested. Don't just reward behavior when you're training. Reward all good behavior even if you haven't asked for it.

Remember that food and toys are primary rewards to a dog because they are things that dogs really want. A few dogs are motivated by praise, but to be honest, not as many as people think. Playtime or a walk are also powerful rewards for good behavior.

The most common problem with rewards is that people often inadvertently reward a dog for the wrong behavior. Say your dog barks when he sees another dog. You think he is afraid, and pet him to try to calm him down. "It's OK," you say. "Nothing bad is going to happen." Look at this from your dog's point of view. He barked and you reinforced his bark, and the emotion behind the bark by giving him your attention, therefore he is more likely to bark again the next time he sees a dog. People often misuse rewards (or corrections for that matter) because they somehow imagine that dogs can tell the difference between good and bad behavior. This is simply not the case. Dogs associate only what they most recently did with the reward or correction. That's why your timing has to be perfect.

If you are using food treats, offer the dog something he's really going to love and that he doesn't get very often. A couple of bits of dry food or kibble is not going to do it. Strips of cooked chicken, beef, or liver, and cubes of cheese will really get him going.

Ration the rewards

Once you have started training, don't reward the dog for every successful action. Always give him praise, but keep the rewards intermittent. This adds value to what you are giving him, and makes him learn faster. If you always reward your dog for a particular sort of behavior, no matter how well he performs it, that behavior is never going to improve, since you have given the dog no feedback about which is better. If the dog thinks he's always going to be rewarded, he may refuse to do anything that doesn't have a reward attached to it. Then it's no longer a reward, but a bribe.

Using clickers

Many dog trainers use clickers, and dogs often respond well to the sound. The important thing to remember if you are using a clicker is to pair the clicking sound with the reward. The click means: "You got it right!" You don't ask a dog to do something by clicking: You confirm that he's about to be rewarded. You should always "charge up" the clicker with a reward. A food treat is good for this.

Corrections

A correction is not a punishment. A correction is simply the way you show the dog he has done something that you don't like or hasn't done something he's been asked to do. I chiefly use vocal corrections. Time out – when you remove your presence from the dog – can also be a potent correction.

One of the least effective of all vocal corrections is "no." From puppyhood onward, most dogs hear the word "no" so often that they must think it's their name. The type of vocal correction I use in training is sounds. They pull the dog up short, and direct his attention to what he's just done.

Never growl at a dog. But if I can see trouble brewing, I sometimes say: "Don't you dare!" in a deep voice and with my eyebrows raised.

Always back up a correction with praise if the dog has listened to the correction. Make it easy for him to do well.

AH AH!

This is a harsh, guttural sound that I use for small misdemeanors, for example, when a dog has put his front paws on the kitchen counter. I may step it up in tone and volume if the action is repeated. I also use it loudly for bigger misdemeanors.

UH OH!

This vocal correction means: "You didn't do what I asked, so I am removing the reward from you for a moment. I will ask you again and will keep removing the reward until you do what I ask." Accompany the sound by removing the reward from sight. You could also say: "Too bad."

IIEE!

Making a yelping sound tells the dog: "Stop mouthing me! That hurts!"

A deep grunt or groan can be used to distract a dog when he's behaving incorrectly. If it is difficult to get a dog's attention, I sometimes use sound diversions. A blast from a horn or two pan lids banged together makes a strong enough sound to stop most dogs for a moment. The object is not to scare them, but to attract their attention, or distract them if an emotion is getting too intense.

Keep this firmly in mind. REWARD behavior you want to encourage. CORRECT or ignore behavior you want to discourage.

Essential training tips

Begin training early, and keep training throughout the dog's life. Normal dogs can start training at seven weeks of age, when their brains are sufficiently developed. Many people think that once dogs have learned what they need to know, the training can stop. It shouldn't. Dogs can and should keep learning all through their lives.

Three sessions of between five and ten minutes a day are recommended for basic obedience training. But keep communicating with your dog all day long.

Only give a signal once. If you repeat cues over and over, you are teaching your dog to sit, for example, on the fourth time you say the word. I like my dogs to respond to my signals the first time I communicate with them. If they don't, they don't get a reward.

Vary your body positions. The dog should respond when you are sitting, crouching, or standing, not just when you are standing and facing him.

Start close and then move farther away. Increase the distance between you and your dog.

Be patient and accept your dog's failures as well as his successes. Some dogs learn slowly. Most of the time, it's three steps forward and one step back.

The secret of positive training is never to manipulate the dog's body physically. The dog should do the mental work to figure out how to get the reward.

Tired dogs don't learn. Mental work can be more tiring than physical activity.

Begin training in a quiet environment – dogs learn faster when there is less around to distract them. Once your dog is responding well, move to a more stimulating environment, then gradually introduce him to other places. I call this "varying the picture." Train around the house first, making use of different rooms. Then train in the backyard, street, car, and park. This ensures that the dog responds everywhere and not just in the kitchen.

Training has to be really solid before it works in places where there are multiple distractions. Trainers call this "proofing." They test the success of their training by asking the dog to respond in situations where there is a lot going on – people stopping to talk, balls being thrown, other dogs running by, and so on.

Training should be as much fun as playing. Dogs get bored easily, so you should adopt an energetic and enthusiastic manner to keep them interested. All sessions should end with plenty of praise.

How to teach your dog commands

In later chapters, I'll be showing you how to teach your dog to walk, to heel, to drop something from his mouth, to give his paw and roll over, and so on. Here, I'm going to focus on a number of basic commands to give you an idea of how the training process works.

The "sit" command

Teaching your dog to sit is a good place to start because it's a natural posture. Do make sure, however, that your dog finds sitting comfortable. If he has bad hips and can't sit for long periods, teach him something different.

Here's what you should do:

Equip yourself with a treat. Hold it between your thumb, index, and third fingers with your palm facing upward.

Call your dog. Puppies learn their names really quickly, and he should come over to investigate.

Show the dog you have a treat in your hand. Hold it in front of his nose. Let him sniff it, lick it, paw it, but don't let him have it.

At this stage, don't utter a command or say anything at all.

Once the dog has more or less learned a command, don't give him a food treat every time he gets it right. Give him a treat every second time, or every third time, or every fifth time. This makes a dog learn faster because he's never sure when you're going to give him a treat. Never phase out treats completely, and always give plenty of praise.

Eventually, your dog will sit. Now here is where you need split-second timing. You have to catch that action and reward it on the spot. Give him the treat and praise him.

Repeat the same procedure two more times. Wait for the action, catch it, give him the treat, and praise him.

The next step is to put in the vocal cue and signal. As your dog is in the act of sitting, say "sit" and raise your wrist slightly. Repeat this five to ten times.

Finally, ask your dog to "sit," using the vocal and hand signal, before he has even started to sit. Repeat the same sequence five to ten times.

If he doesn't "sit" when you ask him to, don't repeat the command. Take the treat immediately out of reach, removing it up to shoulder level, and say "uh oh!" Wait a couple of seconds and try again.

Always give lots of praise after a session.

The "down" command

Once you have taught a dog to sit, you can teach him to lie down. Teaching this command takes a little patience. Very big dogs, such as Great Danes, find lying down and getting up again very strenuous, and I wouldn't recommend making them do it too often.

Here's what you should do:

- Use a treat and put your dog into a sit.

- Place your hand, with the treat in it, palm down on the floor and let your dog sniff it, but don't let him have it. At this stage, don't give a command or say anything at all.

- Your dog will be working out how to get the treat from your hand. As soon as he lies down on his belly, give him the treat and praise him.

- Repeat the same procedure two more times. Wait for the action, catch it, give him the treat, and praise him.

- The next step is to put in the vocal cue and hand signal. As your dog is in the act of lying down, say "down" and lower your hand, palm down, onto the floor. Repeat this five to ten times.

- Finally ask your dog to "down" using the vocal and hand signal before he has even started to lie down.

- If he gets it wrong, say "uh oh!" and repeat the exercise. Release your dog by saying "OK" when you want him to get up again.

The "watch me" command

"Watch me" is an important command, but many people never think about teaching it to their dog. You need to be able to get your dog's attention when you're out and about, if there are children around, or if there are other kinds of distraction that might make him nervous. Here, you follow the same kind of prícedure as you would for teaching him to sit, but you first place the treat in ront of his nose. Then take it up to your eye, holding it between your thumb and index finger—this becomes the hand signal. (Most dogs will look you in the eye if a tasty piece of chicken is dangling beside it.) As when teaching "sit," repeat until he can also respond to the command without a treat.

The "stay" command

The secret of teaching your dog to "stay" is not to move through the stages too fast. Build it up gradually, both lengthening the time and distance. Unlike other commands, you can repeat the "stay" command without undermining the training. That's because you're not asking your dog to take a specific action, and to take it promptly. Instead, you're asking the dog to do nothing at all.

Here's what you should do:

- Put your dog into a sit position and stand in front of him.

- Put your palm near his face and say "stay." Wait a second and reward.

- Repeat and gradually lengthen the time between the command and reward until he is staying for ten seconds.

- Then you can take a step back. If your dog moves to follow you, give a correction – "uh oh!" – and try again.

- Slowly lengthen the distance between you. Always go back to the dog, and don't praise or reward him until you are physically close to him again. Praising from a distance will encourage him to come to you, which undermines what you are trying to teach him.

The "come" command

The "come" command is the most important of all. Start teaching your puppy to come when you call as soon as you bring him home. Teach him to come to you in the house before you try to teach him to come to you outdoors. Make it easy for him to learn by building up from a short distance of about three feet away to greater distances.

Make sure that you are touching your dog before you praise and reward him for coming to you. This tells him that he only gets a reward when he's that close, not a foot or so away.

Puppies naturally like to stay pretty close to their owners. When you start training him to come to you outside, make use of that fact. Let him off the leash and practice the command in the backyard or the park if it's safe to do so.

Sooner or later, however, your dog is going to demonstrate a little more independence. You're out in the park, you call him to come to you, and suddenly he's gone deaf.

A good way of teaching the command and making it fun is to play hide-and-seek. Dogs are good at this game, and really enjoy it. Hide somewhere in the house and call him to come to you. Praise him when he finds you.

Here's what you should do:

Teach him to come to you when you're outside by giving him a jackpot treat. Most dogs, quite rightly, interpret your call to "come" as the end of their fun. That's because they've worked out that when you call them to "come" you usually put them on the leash and take them home. Change your dog's expectations. Call him to "come," give him a food treat, and let him go off and play again. Two treats for the price of one!

Don't just stand there and call your dog to "come." Make yourself more attractive to him by walking or running in the direction you want him to go. Dogs are predisposed to chase, and most will happily play this game. Don't sound harsh or serious when you give the command. Make your voice high and excited. I like to use the kind of chirping, clacking sounds that people use to urge horses to move faster.

Exploit your dog's curiosity. If you don't feel like running, sit or lie down on the ground. Most dogs will come running to find out why you are lying there. Give your dog lots of treats to reassure him that nothing is the matter.

Don't be unreasonable. Your dog is not going to come if he's playing with other dogs. Wait until there's a lull in the action before giving the command.

Never, ever, ever tell a dog off if he is slow in responding to your command to "come." Many owners get anxious or angry in this situation. The very last thing you should do is let him see or hear those negative responses. If you tell him off when he does eventually come to you, you've just taught him not to come when he's called. You have to be a good actor. When he does come to you, however long it takes, praise him.

Never, ever chase a dog when you want him to come to you. However, there may be occasions when you have no option but to run after him. In this case, drop treats behind you as you go, then make your way back to the first treat and hope that, if you have lost him, his nose will lead him back to you.

The "leave it" command

There are many situations when this command is invaluable. The "it" in question may be food that has fallen onto the floor, or it may be a child. Or it may be another dog.

Here's what you should do:

Close your hand around a treat, leaving a little sticking out so that the dog does not have easy access to it. Let him sniff it.

As soon as he pulls his head away from the treat, praise him and give him the treat.

Repeat these steps a couple of times, then add the command "leave it."

As soon as he hesitates or looks away from the treat, praise him and give him the treat.

The next stage is to use two treats. Place a treat in your open hand and repeat the steps, except this time you reward the dog with the treat you have in your other (closed) hand.

Follow this up by putting a treat on the floor. Repeat the process, rewarding your dog with the treat you have in your hand, not the one on the floor.

Finally, put your dog on a leash and walk him past the treat on the floor. As he goes to get the treat, say "leave it." The moment he stops or looks at you, give lots of praise and reward him with the treat that you have in your hand, and not the one on the floor.

Keep repeating the exercise with the dog on the leash. Place other objects on the floor, preferably the type of things you want him to leave alone. It may be the garbage bin, for example. Once your dog is doing well with this command in the house, you can start to use it outside.

Modifying a dog's behavior

Much of what I have discussed in this chapter is concerned with basic obedience training. But there is another aspect to a dog's education and that involves modifying his behavior so that he can live comfortably in our world.

I see a lot of problem dogs in my work, or should I say problem owners? Ninety percent of the time, if a dog has developed a problem with his behavior, it's because he hasn't been handled or treated properly. He hasn't been shown how to cope with the stresses of living in a domestic environment.

Let's take a simple example. Kirsty is a Cocker Spaniel puppy who has developed a bad habit: She eats shoes. In fact, she has eaten her way through several of her owner's most expensive pairs. She chewed the entire back out of a shoe with a designer label while her owner was out at work.

The solution to this "problem" is not obedience training. You can teach a puppy not to chew on inappropriate objects by redirecting him to chew on what he is allowed, but you can't teach him not to chew at all. When puppies are teething, they have an acute need to chew. Poor Kirsty is just seeking a little relief for her sore gums.

The solution is very simple, and that is to keep the shoes away from the dog. Lock them away in a closet where the dog can't get at them. Shoes are very appealing to dogs. They smell powerfully of their owners. But there's something more going on here. Kirsty chewed the shoes, not only to relieve the pain of teething, but because she was upset and lonely when her owner was out at work. She needs to be given both proper chewing toys and a whole lot more attention.

Lack of attention is a cause of many behavioral problems. Whose fault is that?

I will be covering other common problems and their solutions in later chapters. Here, however, I will just say that many of these areas of difficulty can be prevented if you look after your dog properly and manage his environment. Observe him and notice the type of experiences that make him nervous and anxious. It is not always possible or desirable to remove a source of stress completely from a dog's life, but there are various ways in which you can help him meet those situations with more confidence.

Dog's Dinner feeding your dog the right diet

The saying "you are what you eat" is as true for dogs as it is for humans. A good diet keeps a dog healthy and energetic, and makes his coat and eyes shine. A poor diet or one that contains the wrong ingredients can make dogs agitated, aggressive, and hyperactive, as well as fundamentally undernourished.

Half the time we don't know what we are putting into our own bodies, so how can we possibly know what our dogs are getting or what they like to eat? There are so many commercial pet foods on the market, it's hard to choose which one is right for your dog, but how can you tell the difference between what is good food and what is bad? Should you feed wet food or dry food, or a combination of the two? Should you feed your dog human food? How many times a day should you be feeding your dog, and how much? Should you add extra vitamins to your dog's diet? What about dog chews and treats? Should you give your dog a rawhide chew or a beef bone?

So you make your choice. You think you're feeding your dog a nutritious food. It smells good, looks great, and your dog eats it with gusto. Then one day a report is published in the press, and you discover that you have been giving him the equivalent of hamburgers and fries every day.

Unless you take the trouble to investigate what goes into your dog's food, you will never know just how bad some dog food can be. Many of the most popular brands contain ingredients that scientific studies have shown to have adverse physical and mental effects on dogs. Don't be fooled by the fact that your vet may stock the food. Vets are often paid to carry particular brands of food.

As a trainer, one of the first questions I ask owners is what they are feeding their dog. Often, what seems to be exclusively a behavioral problem has a dietary aspect to it. Poor-quality food exacerbates many problems.

The pet food industry is big business. Manufacturers use the same persuaders to sell pet food to us as other companies use to promote the food products we eat ourselves. The packaging is attractive. The brand is well advertised and endorsed. It is also well distributed so you can pick it up almost anywhere – in the supermarket, in the pet store, at the local shop. Price is competitive and affordable. All these factors are bound to influence your choice. They work: That's why companies employ them.

A good diet keeps a dog healthy
and energetic, and makes his coat
and eyes shine.

How to read a list of ingredients

By law, manufacturers have to list what they put in their products. But the list itself can hide a multitude of sins if you don't know how to read it. Many well-known brands of pet food contain chemicals and other unsavory ingredients we wouldn't feed . . . to a dog.

Bear in mind that the ingredient listed first on the packet or label indicates what the food is chiefly made of. Here is a typical list: chicken, chicken by-product meal, cornmeal, ground whole sorghum, ground wholegrain barley, chicken fat, fishmeal, and BHA and BHT.

This list immediately tells me that the food is less than good. Chicken is the first ingredient, and I like the sound of that, but what is chicken by-product meal? What is cornmeal? Why is there added chicken fat? And what is fish doing in the food? What do BHA and BHT stand for? To make it as easy as possible to negotiate this minefield, I'm going to explain exactly what some of these words mean.

Chicken, lamb, or beef
If chicken, lamb, or beef is the first ingredient, then you know that the food contains a decent amount of the clean part of a slaughtered animal. Or does it? If a large portion of the food is made with good cuts of animal meat and the food is not expensive, it is likely that a good percentage of that meat is actually water.

Chicken, beef, or lamb meal
Meal means that the meat has been ground or reduced to small particles. Lamb bone meal is made by drying and grinding bones. These are first sterilized by steam-cooking under pressure.

Chicken by-products
Look away if you're squeamish. By-products include necks, feet, undeveloped eggs, and intestines, including organ meat. Sometimes the head and beak are added. Feathers are allowed, but only those that have slipped in during processing. That's good to know!

Meat by-products
Pet-grade meat by-products consist of parts of any slaughtered animal that are unfit for human consumption, including heads, feet, tails, hair, ligaments, bone, intestines, lungs, and so on. By-products don't necessarily mean that the food is bad. In fact, organ meat is one of the first things a wild dog will eat from the kill. The stomach, intestines, and all its contents are pulled out and eaten first. However, wild organ meat is generally fresh and nutritious, unlike the organ meat that can be used in dog food. We as consumers have no way of knowing if the organs were diseased before they went to the food-processing plant.

Corn, corn gluten, and other cereals

Corn and corn products are difficult for some dogs to digest, as they are for humans. Corn, however, is used liberally in human and dog food as a protein, filler, and sweetener. Some popular dog foods list corn as the first ingredient, even though the product is advertised as "beef and barley." Corn is a cheap protein and fills the food out nicely, but it isn't as nutritious as other foods.

In both humans and dogs, corn is a known allergen. If your dog has been scratching excessively or licking its paws, or has repeated ear infections, too much corn in the diet may be the culprit. Corn can also cause bloating in dogs, which can be very uncomfortable for them.

Wheat can be even more allergenic than corn. Cereal grains that aren't sufficiently processed can also cause allergic reactions.

Digest of beef

This is recovered material from beef carcasses. The "material" is chemically recovered using enzymes. It's not meat; it's everything but. The term may also refer to clean tissue that has not decomposed.

Digest of poultry by-products

Similarly, this is material recovered from poultry carcasses, including heads, feet, and viscera. Fecal and foreign matter isn't supposed to be present in poultry by-products, although it is acknowledged that some of these elements may unavoidably find their way into the food during processing. It just depends how clean the factory is. I bet that makes you feel reassured.

Oils and fats

At the rendering plant, fat is separated from meat using extreme heat and pressure. Then the fat is sprayed onto the food at the end of the processing to make it more palatable. However, the high heat of the rendering process can destroy vital amino acids in the meat protein.

Additives

A wide range of extra ingredients is added to pet food, from vitamins and minerals, to antioxidants, coloring, and preservatives. Vitamins and minerals sound good, don't they? But the reason they have to be added is that processing has often destroyed the vitamins and minerals that were present in the raw ingredients in the first place. That means, in a strange sort of way, that you're effectively paying for them twice over.

Coloring is added to make the food look more appealing – not to the dog, whose color sight is not great, but to his human owner.

Antioxidants such as BHT and BHA and preservatives such as ethoxyquin are chemicals that may adversely affect dog behavior in the same way as junk food and fizzy drinks make children climb the walls. They are in the dog food to give it a longer shelf life.

Many brands of dog food do not even have a sell-by date. What's in those chemicals?

By now, you should be getting the picture. Good-quality dog food – and there are good brands on the market – will not only use decent ingredients, such as a high-quality meat source; it will have been produced in such a way that it retains as much as possible of the basic nutritional value provided by the ingredients. This involves slow cooking at low temperatures under vacuum conditions.

What you should feed your dog

Dogs are omnivores, and they need a varied diet. Like us, they need protein, vitamins and minerals, carbohydrates, and fiber.

An adult dog should gain only about 10% of his total daily calorie intake from protein. This can be either vegetable or animal protein. The dog does not need vast amounts of protein. In fact, too much protein in a dog's diet has been linked with higher levels of aggression. Puppies and older dogs, however, need a higher concentration of protein in their diets. Proteins contain amino acids that are important for growth and health.

Scientific research shows that about 50% of the dog's daily calories can come from carbohydrates.

Fiber is another important part of the dog's diet. Between 2.5% and 4.5% of the dog's daily calories should be in the form of food high in fiber. Fiber helps to prevent diseases such as diverticulitis, and can be an important way of managing conditions such as diabetes and hyperglycemia.

Watch the dog's fat intake. A normal diet can contain 5.5% fat. Too much fat can be positively harmful to some breeds, such as Spaniels, that have a tendency to suffer from pancreatitis. To help their growth, puppies need more fat in their diets than adult dogs.

Essential nutrients include vitamins and minerals. If there are not enough of these nutrients in the diet, the dog may show signs of vitamin or mineral deficiency. Too little sodium, for example, makes dogs overly restless.

Water must be available to the dog at all times. Keep a careful eye on the water bowl in hot weather when dogs drink more.

Avoid supermarket food and mass-market brands, and opt for natural or organic dog foods that are free of chemicals and preservatives. Many of these are relatively low in protein. You can find natural dog food in many of the larger pet stores and in pet health food shops. These foods may seem more expensive than other brands, but they contain far more nutrients and satisfy your dog more readily, so you should not need to feed as much.

Alternatively, you can give your dog human food. I take a lot of trouble over the food I give my foster dogs. Along with a high-quality dog food, I feed them cooked chicken, beef, liver, pasta, rice, potatoes, and cooked vegetables. While I accept that this may be a little more effort than most people are prepared to make, at least ensure you offer your dog the best food you can.

What not to feed your dog

Some human foods are harmful to dogs. This includes chocolate. Never feed a dog chocolate intended for human consumption. In extreme cases, it can kill.

Poultry bones, such as bones from chicken, turkey, and game, are very harmful. They can splinter and tear holes in a dog's intestines and cause life-threatening infections.

If you offer human food, don't give fried food: It is too fatty for dogs. Cook food by poaching and steaming.

I never offer dogs raw meat. I always cook it first, because, unfortunately, these days we can't trust meat to be infection-free in its raw state.

Too much protein in a dog's diet has been linked with higher levels of aggression.

Treats

There are many dog treats on the market, and many of them are no better for your dog than mass-produced dog food. I give strips of cooked chicken, beef, and liver as treats. A marrowbone is a delicious treat for a dog, and is good for his teeth. Dogs are also keen on rawhide chews. This type of chews, however, can give some dogs diarrhea; others may choke on the fragments. I only give a rawhide chew to a dog when I can supervise him. Nylon or dental bones are good for teeth-cleaning.

Wet or dry?

Many people prefer to give their dogs an exclusively dry diet. The reason is usually for their convenience. Dry food doesn't smell so strongly and won't spoil if left out. The feces of dogs fed on dry food are also less smelly. Then there's the argument that dry foods are supposed to keep a dog's teeth in good condition. Really? Think about it. If you ate only biscuits all day long, you'd still have to brush your teeth.

In my experience, an exclusively dry diet can cause problems such as dry skin, excess thirst, stomach pains, flatulence, and bloating. The dog will inevitably drink more and want to pee more, and may have more accidents in the house as a consequence.

On the subject of variety, many people think that dogs don't mind eating the same thing day after day. I couldn't disagree more. By and large, dogs will eat what you put in front of them if they are hungry enough. That tells you nothing about whether they actually enjoy what you're giving them or whether it's doing them any good. Say you feed your dog the same thing every day. What happens when you offer him something different as a treat, a strip of cooked chicken, perhaps? I'd be prepared to bet that he makes it perfectly clear how enjoyable it is to taste something different.

If you consign a dog to a monotonous diet, you are depriving him of sensory exploration and pleasure.

I would always advise a mixed diet of wet and dry food, perhaps with some added vegetables. This gives the dog a variety of tastes and textures.

How often?

I have found that dogs do best when you feed them twice a day, once in the morning and once later in the day toward the end of the afternoon. Puppies up to the age of six months need an extra meal at midday. If you feed your dog only once a day, this can cause both hyperactivity and bloating. Splitting the daily food intake into two meals gives the dog something to look forward to. Dogs have amazing body clocks. They know to within a minute when it's dinnertime. My grandmother always fed her dogs a second meal at 4 pm. As the hour approached, you could swear those Beagles had stopwatches.

I'm not in favor of what is known as "free feeding," when food is on offer at all times. Set meals are easier on the dog's digestive tract. If food is always out, his digestion will be working overtime, around the clock.

Set meals also send out the very clear message that you are in charge of the food. This raises your value in your dog's eyes and makes him more likely to listen to you. Give your dog 20 minutes to finish his food and then take away the remainder.

Always clean your dog's bowl after use. Wash it thoroughly. Dirty bowls are unhygienic and can attract flies.

How much?

Obesity in dogs is just as big a problem as it is in humans. Overfed dogs are subject to many of the same ailments that affect overweight people, including heart disease, diabetes, and joint strain.

It is only possible to give rough estimates with respect to quantity. Obviously, smaller dogs require less food than large dogs. Very active breeds also need more calories than dogs who are content to snooze on your lap for much of the day.

Don't rely completely on manufacturers' guidelines – they're in business to sell you more dog food. Instead, consult breed charts for the recommended weight range for your dog. Weigh him or have him weighed regularly. You'll have to take a large dog to the vet to weigh him. You can weigh a small dog yourself; pick him up and weigh both of you together. To find out how much he weighs, subtract your weight from the combined weight.

Otherwise, it's a question of monitoring your dog. If he's getting plenty of exercise but is still gaining weight, you're feeding him too much. If he's regularly leaving a lot in his bowl after 20 minutes are up, you're offering him too much. If he's lethargic and losing weight, or if he's ravenous at every meal, he may need a calorie boost. A dog is the right weight when you can feel his ribs clearly but can't see them.

Remember that illness or underlying problems such as worms can affect your dog's appetite. A very hungry dog may be a host to parasites. Or he may simply be a greedy little pup. Some dogs are gluttons, and these tend to be the ones who are past masters at persuading us how starving they are! Ask yourself, too, whether food is the only thing the dog has to look forward to in his day. If not much else is happening to give him pleasure, you can be sure he'll be fixated on food.

Manners, please!

Take advantage of meal times to reinforce yourself as the leader. Always fill your dog's bowl on the counter, not on the floor in front of him. As I mentioned before, you can pretend to nibble at his food before you put it down to remind him of your leadership. You are more valuable if you are in control of your dog's most pleasurable resources. I sometimes delay a meal a little from a set time for the same reason. Bear in mind that your dog will work harder for a food treat if he is a little hungry, so don't train directly after a meal.

Your dog should have to work for his food – he would have to do so in the wild. Make him sit and stay until the bowl is on the floor, and then give him the release command "OK."

Feeding problems

Before you go on to tackle any feeding problem that appears on the surface to be behavioral in origin, make sure that you eliminate the possibility of any other underlying cause. The way your dog behaves can be affected by something in his diet, by an illness or condition that you haven't picked up on, or by medication. Always check with your vet what side effects you can expect if your dog is being treated with drugs.

Here are some common feeding problems and how I would go about tackling them.

Another way to make meal times fun for dogs is to play games of hide and seek. Hide food in various locations around the kitchen. That way he really has to work for it. This is not cruel; this is simply providing him with the means to use his senses and express natural hunting behavior.

Problem: Scavenging and stealing

You get up from the breakfast table to answer the phone, and when you get back you find that your dog has helped himself to the remains of your half-eaten toast. Worse, there are bite marks in the butter.

Or, you settle yourself down for a good night's sleep and just as you are about to drop off to sleep there's a resounding crash from the kitchen. You rush downstairs, fearing a burglar has broken in, and discover that your own four-legged sneak thief has managed to tip over the garbage and is happily gorging himself on the contents.

One day your neighbor drops by for a visit, bringing her three-year-old daughter with her. Little Ruby is treated to a cookie and then toddles off happily to play with your dog. The next minute, Ruby is wailing and the cookie is halfway down your dog's throat.

Solution: Keep food out of the reach of dogs

If your dog is regularly stealing or scavenging food, it's not *his* problem, it's *yours*. You have to manage your environment so that the dog does not get the chance to eat what you don't want him to.

We expect dogs to have incredible control over their impulses, much better control than we would have in similar circumstances. Just think how powerful the dog's sense of smell is.

Then imagine what a temptation food represents when it is lying around unattended. Dogs will jump onto chairs and up onto tables to get to food. If they're big enough, they'll jump up onto kitchen counters and happily graze away. They'll knock over garbage cans to get at the contents that smell so enticing to them.

To you, what's in the can is garbage. That's not the dog's perception. If your dog gets into the rubbish, he may well eat something, like a chicken bone, that could do him a great deal of harm.

Put food away. Lock your can in a cupboard or choose a can that can only be opened with a catch. Make it easy for your dog to succeed. And never, ever punish or correct him when you come into the room and discover he has polished off the pasta. He won't have the first idea what you are punishing him for. By now, the pasta is long gone.

When a dog snatches food from the hand of a child, it's more serious. Children who are not used to dogs may be very frightened by the experience and may even be hurt if the dog has been a little hasty. Small children also like to tease dogs with food, without realizing what a temptation this presents for even the best-trained dog. Prevention is always better in this situation. Children are much closer to dogs in height than adults. The food they hold is much closer to the floor, which is a dog's feeding level. Explain to your friend and to the child that while the dog is around it is better to eat the cookie sitting at the table.

If you can spot your dog about to snatch food from someone's hand, use the command "leave it" (see page 88 for how to teach this command). The same command is invaluable when you are walking your dog and there is garbage all over the sidewalk or chicken bones discarded in the park.

If the snatching took place behind your back, however, there is nothing you can do in the way of punishment or correction. You can only correct a dog effectively within one second of the wrong or undesired behavior.

Problem: Your dog has something in his mouth you don't want him to have

We try to be vigilant when we are walking our dogs, but sometimes it isn't possible to spot every hazard. Anyone who walks dogs regularly in cities and urban parks will recognize the lurking menace of discarded chicken bones. Fried chicken is a popular fast food. Equally common, unfortunately, is the disgusting habit of dropping the bones on the ground. Litterbugs are not merely despoiling our environment, they're putting the lives of our dogs at risk. Chicken bones are lethal.

Perhaps what your dog has got his teeth around is not as dangerous as a chicken bone. But you still don't want him to have it. What do you do?

Solution: The "take it and drop it" game

Most of the time when a dog has something in his mouth, you have to accept that it now belongs to the dog, particularly when that something is food. Even a pack leader will not challenge a dog of lower status over a piece of meat. How would we feel if someone reached into our mouth and grabbed food out of it?

If your dog has gotten hold of a piece of bread, it's best to let him eat it. If it's a chicken bone, however, you can't afford to take the risk.

Try to get the bone out of the dog's mouth by prying open his jaws. Dogs have very strong jaws, and you will need to be very careful not to get yourself bitten in the process. If you have a delicious treat on hand – some cooked chicken or liver – you may be able to get your dog to relinquish the bone himself. But it has to be a higher trade.

You stand a better chance of success of getting a dog to drop something from his mouth if you have trained him from an early age that dropping objects can be fun and a source of pleasure.

Here's what you should do:

Equip yourself with five or so different toys that your dog likes. Try to choose his favorites. Each toy should be slightly higher in value than the one before; that is, it should be more interesting to the dog.

The first step is to teach your dog the command "take it." Out of those five objects, choose the toy that has the lowest value as far as your dog is concerned. Call your dog and show him the object. As he begins to open his mouth to take it, say "take it." Then when he has taken the toy, praise him.

Let him have some time with the toy, running and playing.

Now you get another toy of slightly more interest to the dog and put it in your other hand. Call your dog and show him the object. A dog will naturally relinquish something that he perceives as plain OK for something he sees as better. As soon as he drops the first object, say "drop it." Then praise him. Immediately give him the other object and say "take it." Praise him when he does.

Then leave him to play a while with the second object.

Repeat the "take it and drop it" game until you reach the last object. Make sure it's a real bonus for the dog. A rawhide chew, perhaps.

Allow him to chew on the hide for a while, then produce another rawhide chew. Say "drop it" to ask him to drop the chew he has in his mouth, and say "take it" as you offer him the second one. This teaches him to give up high-value, tasty things as well.

Problem: Food guarding

Food is a very important resource to a dog. It guarantees his survival. But some dogs are more prone to guarding their food than others. They growl when you come anywhere near their bowls. In extreme cases, they may lash out and nip or bite. This can be serious when there are children in the family. I always say: "Let eating dogs eat." If your dog is protecting his food excessively, however, you need to take further action.

Solution: Teach your dog that you are the source of his food, not a threat

One of the best ways of dealing with this problem is to prevent it in the first place. I always try to train puppies that whenever I'm around their food bowl, good things happen.

When I'm feeding puppies, I don't prepare their food on the counter and then set it down in front of them. I put an empty bowl on the floor and I sit beside it. Then I start putting food into the bowl a little bit at a time. The puppy, of course, will make a beeline for the food. While he eats, I'll continue to sit by the bowl, adding food bit by bit. This teaches the puppy that I am their food source and not a threat.

Eventually, I will set the puppy's bowl down on the floor with food already in it. But I will reinforce the message by dropping food – a piece of chicken, for example – into the bowl from time to time.

If food-guarding is a problem in an adult dog, you can take similar steps to teach him that you are no threat to his food, but that your presence near his bowl means that good things happen to him. Please note that small children should never be allowed to do this type of training.

Here's what you should do:

Prepare the dog's food in the usual way.

Then set down an empty bowl. The dog will go for the bowl, see there is nothing in it, and look at you.

As he looks at you, praise him and throw a little food into the empty bowl from a distance. He will eat it. Then throw in a little bit more. Repeat this until he has finished his meal.

Make no attempt to pick up the bowl before he has finished.

For the next month, continue to throw food into the empty bowl at every single meal. For the first week, keep on doing this from a distance. Then gradually move closer until you are able to stand right by him. Always praise him when he looks up at you, then add food to his bowl.

Never push a dog too fast. If he begins to guard at any stage, move back a step in your training.

Try approaching his bowl from different directions, always keeping food in your hand. Varying the picture in this way will help your dog feel relaxed if his bowl is approached from different angles and by different people.

The last stage is to touch your dog as you throw food into the bowl. First, you touch him for a second, then gradually work up to a small stroke. You might even try touching his bowl. Be careful with this. Only touch his bowl as if by accident when you are putting the food in.

Accidents Will Happen

how to house-train your dog

House-training is a vital part of raising a puppy, and has to be done consistently to be effective. And when it comes to house-training, a positive approach works really well. What do I mean by a positive approach? I mean one that focuses on preventing accidents, instead of waiting for them to happen. I mean making it easy for your dog to succeed by managing your environment – you need to play an active role. You should never blame a dog when he fails.

My husband and I have fostered many shelter dogs, both puppies and adults, taking them into our home and rehabilitating them so they can be adopted by new owners. The first thing we do is to house-train them properly. A puppy is easier to train than an adult dog that hasn't received proper guidance when it was younger. While the training takes longer for an adult dog, it can still be done.

What follows is a guide to successfully house-training a puppy or adult dog. There are a number of ways in which this can be achieved, depending on your circumstances and the age of the dog. Paper training is good for puppies that have not yet been vaccinated and that are therefore unable to go outside until they are fully protected from infection. It is also the best method for people who live in an apartment or do not have a backyard of their own. Crate training is another option.

How often?

An eight-week-old puppy can hold on for one to two hours before he needs to relieve himself, provided he is awake but at rest. By three months, that period of control should extend to two to three hours – as a general rule, an hour of control is added for every month of a puppy's age. Exercise, excitement, feeding, or waking from a nap reduces this period. When you first start house-training a puppy, whatever method you choose, bear in mind that he needs to go an average of eight times a day.

If you leave food out for the dog all day long, he will need to go more, and it will be harder to get him into a routine. Once you control access to food, eliminations will become much more regular. Regardless of how many times a day you feed your dog, leave the food down for 20 minutes only. If he doesn't eat it all by the end of that time, pick it up and don't offer any more until the next feed. He will learn that he has to eat his food when you put it down for him.

Once you control access to food, eliminations will become much more regular.

Paper training

If you have a very young puppy that is not yet vaccinated, and if you do not have access to a private yard, paper training is the best option. Many people attempt to house-train a puppy using newspaper, but newspaper does not absorb urine sufficiently and small dogs that are long-haired tend to get wet after urinating because they are low to the ground. I prefer to use special paper pads that you can obtain from pet stores. These absorb urine very well and are also scented in such a way as to attract puppies to urinate on them. They are also great to chew!

If you don't want to use pads, you need to remove the puppy from the newspaper right after he has relieved himself to prevent him from tracking urine around the home. Most dogs have a tendency to turn around and sniff what they have done (we humans also inspect what we produce), so you'll have to catch him on the spot. In either case, whether or not you are using paper or pads, keep your puppy's hair short around the anal area and wash him regularly to remove excess dirt.

Where to put the paper

Just as you would not allow a baby to crawl around your home unsupervised, particularly a baby not wearing a diaper, you need to restrict a puppy to a single area while you are training him. If you don't, you're just asking for trouble. Choose a room that has a floor that is easily cleaned. In many cases, this will be the kitchen. Puppy-proof the area thoroughly. Remove any articles lower down that the puppy might be able to damage or chew. Pay particular attention to electrical cords and unplug any cords or appliances from floor-level sockets to prevent the risk of electrocution. Open windows only from the top, so the puppy does not stray outdoors or fall from an upper story, either accidentally or if he sees a cat or some other enticing temptation. Use a system of baby gates or fences to keep the puppy in the safe area,

but don't isolate him from the rest of the family in a distant room behind a closed door. He should be able to see you, hear you, and be part of the family.

To begin with, line the whole safe area with pads and see where the puppy likes to go. He will soon find a favorite place, and the scent will keep attracting him back to the spot. Dogs do not like to foul their nest, so he is likely to choose an area that is away from where he sleeps and eats.

Once he has chosen his spot, you can start removing the pads, taking away one every couple of days until there are only two pads left. If your puppy has a good aim, you might be able to make do with only one pad. However, puppies often feel the pads under their feet and then place their rear ends facing the other way over the floor, so a bigger area is often more practical. Change the pads regularly.

Rewards

Your puppy needs to know that each time he relieves himself on the pad or newspaper (or outside), he gets praised and given delicious treats. You must praise him as soon as he has finished. Say "good boy" and give him a fabulous treat like a piece of chicken. At this stage, reserve that special chicken treat only for successful elimination rather than for any other good behavior. What you are doing is building up a positive association between a reward and elimination that takes place in front of you, whether it is on the paper or outside.

Here's the scenario:

 The puppy goes to his paper.

 As he relieves himself, you say, very quietly, "go wee," or whatever you feel comfortable saying, as long as it is exactly the same words every time.

 As soon as he has finished, praise him by telling him what a good boy he is and give him the chicken treat. Play with him.

 Everyone in the family should follow suit each time they see the puppy go.

Corrections

Never, ever correct your dog if you come across the results of an accident after the event has taken place. If you don't catch him in the act, it is pointless correcting him. Dogs only associate a correction with a behavior within one second of that behavior taking place. If you come home to see an accident on the floor and punish him, you are really punishing him for coming up to welcome you.

Many owners tell me that their dog knows he has done wrong because he looks guilty as soon as they walk through the door. Well, he might look guilty, but that's only because he's scared at the way you are behaving toward him. He's picked up your negative body signals or your groan of exasperation. As far as he's concerned, he had done nothing wrong. It takes only one such inappropriate correction to make a puppy worry every single time you come in through the door. In his mind, you are angry with him for coming up to you, not for the mess on the floor. He will start to distrust you because he will be unsure when a punishment for no reason is going to come next.

Please remember that punishing a puppy or dog by pushing his nose in what he has done is wrong. It teaches him nothing except that you are the source of unpleasant experiences.

If you catch your puppy eliminating inside and not on his pad, say "ah!" firmly, pick him up mid-pee (he will stop), and take him to his pad (or when he has gone outside a couple of times, you can take him straight outdoors). Wait for him to finish, and praise him, giving chicken as a reward. You are now beginning to show him that relieving himself in the right place brings great things.

Crate training

Crate training is much more popular in the United States than it is in Britain. It is also more popular for people who live in apartments in urban environments. Crates are a good house-training aid, *provided* they are used correctly. They become a problem when owners use them as a punishment area, where a puppy can be confined if he has done something wrong, or as a means of keeping a dog from chewing on the furniture when the owner is out. If you isolate a dog in a crate for a large portion of the day while you are at work, he will literally go crazy when you come home in the evening and let him out. What would you do if you were shut in a small cage for eight hours?

Crate training exploits the fact that dogs are clean animals and do not like to sleep where they have soiled. It therefore enhances bladder control by encouraging a puppy to wait until he is out of the crate to relieve himself. You have to spot the signs that he needs to go and either take him outside immediately or take him to his pad.

The crate is an enclosed cage made of plastic or metal wire that is just big enough for a puppy or dog to stand up, turn around, and lie down in. Any bigger, and the dog will choose an area at the far end of the crate to relieve himself. You can buy either a large crate, blocking part of it off for the time being, or use a succession of crates of increasing size as your puppy grows. If you are going to use a crate, you must use it as a house-training tool only. When your dog is house-trained, you can pack away the crate and give him a normal bed. Or, if he likes his crate, make sure the door is always open so he can come and go as he pleases.

I once advised a family that was keeping their young female Jack Russell shut in a crate for nine hours at a time. Jack Russells are naturally active and, like all Terriers, have a tendency to be bossy. Skippy's confinement made her so frustrated that when she was eventually released from the crate at the end of the day, she turned into a tornado of fury, with most of her aggression directed against the family's older dog. That's the wrong use of a crate.

A small puppy has limited bladder control. If you leave him in the crate too long, you will be forcing him to soil his bed and that is unkind. If he is continually forced to soil his bed, he might never become house-trained because eventually he won't care where he goes. He also needs to be physically active and to be socializing with his family, not stuck in the crate for long periods.

Getting your puppy used to the crate

I like to use the crate with the door open. If I am not there to supervise, I will shut the door. It takes a couple of days for a puppy to feel comfortable in the crate, so you must introduce it to him slowly. If you do that properly, the crate becomes a happy place for the puppy to be, like a den. He will see that it is warm, comfortable, and that it contains his favorite toys. I sometimes feed the puppy his meals in the crate to reinforce the idea that good things happen there.

When you introduce the crate, let the puppy go in and explore it. After he's had a chance to explore it thoroughly, close the door for a second and open it again, giving the puppy a lot of praise. Toss a tasty treat into the crate, let the puppy retrieve it, then shut the door for 30 seconds. When you open the door, praise him. Repeat this exercise until your puppy is happy to spend five minutes in his crate. Then leave the door open and begin again the next day. Gradually you will arrive at the point where the puppy is going in and out by himself and is happy to be in the crate, whether or not the door is closed.

If you are crate training your puppy, do not leave him shut in the crate for more than three hours at a time. He may well choose to be in it for longer if the door is open.

Some puppies or dogs never take to crate training and will become anxious when placed in the crate. Excessive whining, barking, chewing on the wire, scraping, or urinating will tell you that the crate is not a good tool to use. It doesn't mean your dog won't become house-trained. I have house-trained many dogs without using a crate at all.

My preferred set-up

When I am house-training a puppy or a dog, I give him a safe area of his own. In my case, this is the kitchen. I use a baby gate so the dog does not have access to other areas of the house. The area is completely puppy- and dog-proofed, so I can leave him safely in this area unsupervised. There is a crate in one corner, and I feed the dog nearby.

If I am paper training, the pads are a distance away from the crate. If I am not paper training a puppy, but taking him directly outside, there is no paper in the safe area at all and the crate is simply the place where the puppy or dog sleeps.

I leave the crate door open so that the puppy can come and go as he pleases, except when he is first learning bladder control. Then I will shut the door for short periods throughout the day when I am not there to supervise. If I am out for more than an hour at a time, the puppy is left to roam free. Once the puppy is older, he can hold on for longer and can spend longer periods in the crate.

Because young puppies need to be close to their owners, especially at bedtime when they are more likely to feel vulnerable, I also have a night crate in my bedroom. That way I can hear if the puppy needs to go in the night and, at the same time, he feels safe with me close by. After a week or so, I move his night crate from my bedroom into the hall. After a little while longer, I do without the second crate and the puppy sleeps in the kitchen. It takes a couple of weeks to make this transition. During the night, the crate is closed but it is up to me to take the puppy out to pee once or twice a night if he needs it. As the puppy gets older, he will develop better bladder control and will sleep through the night without needing to eliminate at all.

Training your dog to relieve himself outside

When you train your dog to relieve himself outside, it is important that you stick to a routine. You can also use the schedule given on the next page for paper training during the period when your puppy is not yet protected from infection by his vaccinations. Instead of taking your puppy out for a walk, take him to the paper. Six weeks of house-training and no accidents in the house means your dog is pretty well house-trained.

If you have a backyard, you can take your dog outside at regular intervals or whenever you spot the signs that he needs to go. But don't just let the puppy out by himself. He'll want to come in again to be with you. Go outside with him and give him lots of praise and a treat when he does what he's supposed to do. If you live in an apartment, training a puppy to go outside can be a little more difficult because you won't be able to respond quite so quickly.

6:30 am: Puppies naturally need to go as soon as they wake up. Take him for a walk or accompany him outside. He should urinate and might defecate. Play with him for a while and then supervise him the whole time if he is out of his safe area, or put him in his safe area if you are unable to supervise him.

8:30 am: Give the puppy his first meal. Leave food for 20 minutes and take him out after he has finished eating. He should urinate and might defecate. Play with him for a while and then supervise him the whole time if he is out of his safe area, or put him in his safe area if you are unable to supervise him.

10:30 am: Take your puppy out again to urinate. Play with him for a while and then supervise him the whole time if he is out of his safe area, or put him in his safe area if you are unable to supervise him.

1 pm: Give the puppy his second meal. Take him out. He should urinate and defecate. Only take him for a good walk once he has urinated. Play with him for a while and then supervise him the whole time if he is out of his safe area, or put him in his safe area if you are unable to supervise him.

4 pm: It is better to feed a puppy at this time rather than later in the evening. After feeding, take him out. He should urinate and might defecate. Play with him for a while and then supervise him the whole time if he is out of his safe area, or put him in his safe area if you are unable to supervise him.

6 pm: Take him out again to urinate. Play with him for a while and then supervise him the whole time if he is out of his safe area, or put him in his safe area if you are unable to supervise him.

9 pm: Take him out again. He needs to eliminate before he goes to bed so he should defecate as well as urinate. Limit water after this walk unless it is really hot. If so, give him ice cubes, which allow him to get his water slowly.

While you are adhering to this schedule, you can also use the crate at various times of the day. Young puppies need a lot of naptime, but make sure you are not overusing the crate.

When your puppy starts to get better control, you can begin to cut down on the number of times you take him out. An adult dog still needs to eliminate on average four times a day.

Your dog will defecate at different times of the day. There are no rules as to when he should go, but note when it happens so you can tell when he might be more likely to go in the future. Cutting down to two meals a day will alter the times when he defecates.

Getting him used to going outside

If you began by paper training your puppy, take some soiled paper out with you with his scent on it. Put that paper, along with a clean one, on the ground. Choose an area that is relatively private and quiet, by a wall, lamppost, or a designated area in your yard. Let the puppy walk around and sniff the paper. Tell him to "go wee" in a soft, kind voice. When he does, praise him and give him chicken or a similar treat.

Gradually decrease the size of the paper until he doesn't need it anymore. Remember that the feel of the paper or pad under his feet is very different from the feel of concrete or grass, both in temperature and texture. To get him used to concrete or grass, get a concrete slab or a tray full of grass and put it under the paper or pad in his safe area.

Pick up!

Take a supply of bags with you when you go out so that you can clean up after your dog. There are special scented plastic ones you can buy, or biodegradable eco-alternatives. Or you can use paper towels. When I was a dog-walker, there was a place on Wimbledon Common called "Poo Corner." This area surrounded the car park. People would drive up, let their dogs out, and the dogs would defecate before going for their walk. Hardly anyone cleaned up after their dogs. When children came to play on the Common after school, they had to pick their way through a minefield of dog excrement to get there. Not picking up after your dog in a public area is lazy and unhealthy for all other users of that area. There are no excuses. Pick up after your dog!

Take a supply of bags with you when you go out so that you can clean up after your dog.

Be prepared for accidents

Please be tolerant of accidents. There will be some, and it's important to be patient and not undo all the good work you have done by getting angry.

Any urine in the house that hasn't been cleaned up thoroughly is an open invitation to a dog to go again on the same spot. You need to use a biological cleanser to remove the enzymes in the urine so there is no lingering scent.

House-training problems

One of the most frequent "behavior problems" I encounter in dogs, particularly those whose owners live in apartments, is inappropriate elimination. It is a problem that drives people to the brink of insanity and dogs into confinement.

But think about it for a moment. Why do we call inappropriate elimination a behavior problem? Elimination is necessary for health because it removes bodily wastes and toxins. It's entirely natural. Whether the dog has gone in a place that is appropriate or inappropriate is your judgment, not his.

One of the first things I ask my clients is to describe their dog's elimination habits. I can learn a lot about a dog's physical and mental health by what, how, and when he eliminates. You'd be surprised how often this gives me a clearer picture of another seemingly unrelated problem.

Whether your dog has peed in a place that is appropriate or inappropriate is your judgment, not his.

Problem: Accidents from a house-trained dog

Your dog is house-trained, but has started to have the occasional accident indoors. Does this mean he has forgotten his training?

Solution: Treat the underlying cause

If the accidents only happen very infrequently, then the most likely explanation is that you haven't been around when the dog needed to go out. If you leave your dog for long periods – and you shouldn't – sooner or later he is going to need to relieve himself. Even a well-trained dog will have an accident in these circumstances. Don't tell him off. He won't know why you are punishing him. Besides, it's your fault, not his.

If the accidents are happening with greater frequency, there are a number of other possible causes for the behavior. These include:

Illness

If your dog is urinating or messing frequently indoors, it could be the sign of a health problem. The dog may have picked up an infection, eaten bad food, or there might be some other physical cause. If you notice a sudden change in your dog's elimination habits, you should take your dog to the vet without delay, if possible taking a stool sample with you.

Fear

We all know that fear can cause humans to lose control of their bodily functions. I have seen the same thing happen with dogs. Some experts maintain that by eliminating, the dog makes himself lighter so that he can run away from danger more easily.

Dogs that suffer from intense separation anxiety will also defecate and urinate out of stress. A telltale sign that this is the underlying cause is when a dog defecates or urinates right by the door of the room where you have shut him in (or on the other side of the door where you have shut yourself in). See page 192 for ways to treat this kind of anxiety.

Submission

Submissive urination is also very common and is thought to be an important signal in dog communication. The more submissive dog will pee in deference to the more dominant one and, in doing so, will communicate that he is not a threat. In the same way, dogs may urinate when a stranger strokes them. As usual, we humans often misread this signal and may respond with anger when a dog urinates in this way. This, of course, makes the situation much worse.

If your dog pees when he is greeted by you or someone else, don't get angry and correct him. Instead, take the pressure off him by saying a simple "hello." Then ignore him until he has calmed down and become more comfortable in your presence or in the presence of a guest. Greet him carefully and praise him when he is calm and does not pee. Make sure all your family and visitors to your home do the same. If you correct a dog in this situation, he may become too frightened to pee in front of you when you take him out for a walk.

Excitement

The same physiological process can occur when a dog is overly excited. This normally happens when greeting a human or another dog, but it can happen during vigorous play. Again, don't overreact or make a big deal out of it.

Age

Elderly dogs sometimes lose control of bladder function or become incontinent. A thorough examination by your vet is needed if your dog is getting on in years and shows any signs of incontinence.

Problem: You can't seem to train your puppy to relieve himself outside

Your puppy has had his lunch. He's showing signs that he's ready to go. You get his leash and take him out for a walk. Twenty minutes later, he still hasn't gone. You think he must not need to go this time and you take him home. No sooner do you get through the door than he has an accident.

Solution: Break the pattern

Dogs are at their most vulnerable when they are eliminating, which is why they choose the spot with care. If you live in a busy city, your puppy may not feel comfortable relieving himself outside. He may only feel safe enough to do this indoors.

You need to break the habit by teaching your puppy that he only gets the fun of a walk after he has eliminated. Give your dog confidence by taking him to a safe, quiet place to eliminate and provide him with good experiences when he does.

After he has finished his meal, take him out and wait for him to go. If he doesn't produce anything after 10 minutes, bring him back in, and then turn around and go straight back out again. Repeat this until he has eliminated outside. Then he gets praise, a treat, and his walk. If it takes all day, it takes all day. Break the pattern once, and you won't have to break it again.

I was once faced with a six-month-old puppy that wouldn't eliminate outside. I took that puppy in and out again for nine hours. In and out. In and out. In and out. Eventually she got the message and an enormous amount of praise. After that, she and her owners never looked back.

Problem: Scent-marking

Your dog is marking furniture or other areas in the home with his scent.

Solution: Neutering or resuming house-training

Scent-marking is a vital communication tool for dogs. Dogs mark territory so that other dogs can gain important information about them. Female dogs in heat will also signal their availability in this way.

Does your male dog lift his leg to pee? Clever dog to leave his "calling card" at nose height! Kicking out the back legs spreads the scent of the urine as well as releasing sweat from the glands in the back feet. The dog is saying: "I'm an unfixed male, I'm two feet tall, I've got big teeth and a white bushy tail. I like chicken, bones and chasing a ball. Stay off my patch."

Marking can become a problem when a dog wants to mark territory indoors as well. This tends to arise in un-neutered dogs. Normally, males will no longer scent-mark once they have been neutered and spayed females will have no urge to advertise their period of heat. If a male dog has become accustomed to marking over a long period of time, however, neutering may not do the trick. In this case, you need to resume house-training. Start the whole process all over again.

You'll Never Walk Alone exercising your dog

Exercise is a powerful stress-reliever for all animals. Giving your dog regular walks and runs in the park will enhance his life immeasurably. Of course, there are lots of other ways of exercising your dog, and I'll be covering those in a later chapter. Here, however, I'm going to focus on walking because it is such an important part of the daily routine. One good long walk every day is essential for your dog.

Why? Let's look at it from the dog's point of view. A walk not only exercises him physically, it provides a different environment that challenges his mind and stimulates his senses. Unlike the wolf or the wild dog, the domesticated dog lives in an environment that lacks sensory stimulation, at least of the kind he particularly enjoys.

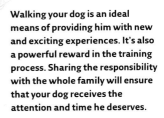

Walking your dog is an ideal means of providing him with new and exciting experiences. It's also a powerful reward in the training process. Sharing the responsibility with the whole family will ensure that your dog receives the attention and time he deserves.

How much exercise is enough?

All adult dogs need to be taken out every day for three short ten-minute walks so they can relieve themselves. In addition to that, they need a good run or walk in the park or some other safe open space.

How much exercise your dog needs will depend on his age and breed. Puppies should not be over-exercised while their bones and muscles are still growing. For example, it is recommended that they should not be taken to agility classes – where they might have to jump over obstacles – until they are 18 months old. Older dogs should not be over-exercised, either. This does not mean consigning them to a sedentary lifestyle, it just means slowing the pace a little, particularly if your aging dog has trouble with his joints, as many do.

Different breeds vary in their need for physical exercise. Size alone is no indication. Small dogs that have been bred to be companions primarily, such as Cavalier King Charles Spaniels, do not need strenuous workouts, although they still need good exercise and sensory stimulation. Terriers, however, who are also small, are very much more active. Working dogs bred for their stamina, such as Collies, which are capable of herding sheep all day without tiring, also need much more exercise than other breeds. Adapt your dog's exercise routine to the type of activity he was bred to perform, whether this is tracking, hunting, retrieving, or herding.

Quality can be just as important as quantity. Running your dog in the same area of the same park every day will be just as monotonous for the dog as it will be for you. Go to different locations within the park or visit a different park. Vary the route you take to get there. Small adjustments can make a lot of difference to the pleasure the dog receives from the outing. All those lovely new smells to smell!

You will know if your dog is not getting enough exercise in one of two ways. If he is gaining weight, he needs to be walked more often and for longer. If he is showing signs of negative behavior, he may not be gaining sufficient stimulation outside the home. Inactive dogs may become destructive or display their anxiety and frustration through chewing, soiling, or barking excessively. Dogs that are left alone for long periods on a regular basis cannot be blamed for taking out their boredom and loneliness on the couch. Chewing relieves stress. It's the same as you biting your nails.

Leaving your dog in the yard all day without taking him for a walk is just as bad as leaving him in the house. The yard might initially be a more stimulating place for him than the kitchen, but after a while it quickly becomes just another room in your house.
If your dog spends long hours at home by himself during the day, consider hiring a dog-walker or take your dog to a reputable doggy daycare center.

Tips for walking your dog

Make sure that the collar and leash fit correctly so that you have control of your dog at all times when you are walking him.

Always keep your dog on the leash until you get to the park or any other space where it is safe for him to run free – you owe it to your dog and to other people and animals around you. Respect the fact that some people do not like dogs or are afraid of them, especially if they see one that is off the leash. And even a well-trained animal is not able to resist certain strong temptations. One second he's by your side, the next he's under a car because he saw a squirrel across the road. I have seen it happen.

In the same way, think very carefully before letting your dog off the leash near water. Every year there are tragic accidents when dogs fall into a river or get swept out to sea and their owners drown in the attempt to rescue them.

Take a supply of bags to clean up after your dog.

Make sure that your dog has all his current identification and license tags fixed to his collar in case of loss or injury. Many owners have their dogs microchipped. This is a simple, relatively painless procedure done at the vet in which a small microchipped disc is inserted under the dog's skin, usually between his shoulders. The disc gives a dog his own unique barcode. If he gets lost and is separated from his collar and tags, the barcode will ensure that he is reunited with you.

If you are walking in a poorly lit area, wear reflective gear and put reflective tags on your dog's leash and collar. This will help drivers see you.

In very hot weather, it is better to walk in the early morning and evening. Dogs can heat up quickly, since they are closer to hot concrete. Dogs that spend a lot of the time indoors may have more sensitive foot pads that can be easily burned. Walk on the shady side of the street. Take a bottle of water so that you can give your dog a drink when he needs it.

Don't let your dog drink from any puddles, as they could contain antifreeze. Antifreeze has a sweet taste that is very alluring to dogs. Even a small amount can kill.

Avoid areas that you suspect have been sprayed with insecticides or chemicals, as these, too, can have potentially harmful effects on your dog.

In cold weather, make sure that you wipe your dog's feet after the walk to get rid of any road salt. This will prevent your dog from ingesting it when he licks his paws.

Walking equipment

When I was employed as a dog-walker, I must have been quite a sight. Every day I would go out with my canine charges, laden down with leashes, collars, halters, harnesses, treat bags, and poop bags. To say nothing of the first-aid kit and the coats for the short-haired dogs in case it got cold.

Dog-walking equipment comes in a huge range of types, from standard leashes and collars, to other devices designed to provide owners with quick fixes. We humans do like a quick fix. Whether it is the cleaning product that promises to take the place of elbow grease or the choke collar designed to teach your dog not to pull, we are very attracted to such apparently easy and effortless solutions. In many cases, there is a cost to be paid. In dog training, the cost is to your dog. A choke chain teaches your dog not to pull by hurting him. Only very experienced trainers can use them properly. I'm an experienced trainer, but I don't like them at all.

Types of leashes

Nylon or cotton leashes

These come in a variety of colors, widths, and lengths. The size of your dog will determine which width of leash you get, with the wider ones being more suitable for larger, heavier animals. Length is another variable. If the leash is too short, it will be too tight and tense and your dog will be more likely to pull; if it is too long, you won't have sufficient control. I use a six-foot leash for walking in public areas.

Leather leashes

These can be flat, rolled, or plaited for additional strength. Leather hardens when it gets wet and may become brittle once it has dried. You might not realize that the leash has weakened until the day it snaps. Dogs like to chew on leather and some may attempt to get at the leash while they are walking in order to do this.

Chain leashes

Because metal doesn't taste or feel as good as cotton, nylon, or leather, these leashes are often used to discourage dogs from jumping and chewing on their leashes while they are being walked. However, these leashes can hurt your hands and can also slip easily through them, which means they are not the safest or the most comfortable to use. It is better to teach your dog not to bite on the leash and purchase a more comfortable one.

Extendable leashes

Designed to give the dog a little extra freedom, the extendable leash comes in a variety of lengths (12-foot and 30-foot are the most common). It is important that you choose the right leash for your dog's weight. Usually the maximum recommended weight will be indicated on the packaging or leash. Shorter extendables can snap if used on a heavier dog. Because the extendable leash reduces your control over your dog, don't use it to walk a dog along roads where there is the risk of traffic or in heavily populated areas, where it could trip people up. I prefer to teach a dog that walking close to me is better than walking far out in front. Extendables do not help to teach this.

Stretch leashes

Like extendables, stretch leashes are designed to give the dog more freedom. They come in different styles and materials. Some look like curly telephone wires. I have never used one in my dog-training work. Stretch leashes can stretch farther than they are supposed to, which could be dangerous if your dog makes a sudden lunge. It's better to teach your dog to walk correctly on a normal leash.

Slip leashes

A slip leash has a ring at one end. When the leash is threaded through the ring, it doubles up as a slip collar. Slip leashes provide little control and can choke a dog if he makes a sudden lunge. The only time I use one is when I am working with a particularly sensitive or aggressive dog that does not like being handled around the head.

Types of collars

Flat nylon or cotton collars

In my opinion, a flat-buckle nylon or cotton collar is the best collar you can use. Leather tends to harden when it gets wet. Nylon and cotton collars are durable, washable, dry easily, and are generally less harsh on the dog's skin. Cotton tends to be softer than nylon. A buckle is better than a plastic-snap fastener, which can come apart if your dog makes a sudden lunge. How wide the collar should be depends on how big your dog is. In general, a collar should be wide enough to distribute pressure evenly. A Retriever, for example, needs a collar that is approximately one inch in width. If your dog pulls, then a rolled collar is not as safe as a flat one because it covers less surface area on your dog's neck.

Choke chains and collars

How shall I put this nicely? I hate them! The reason why I will not use them is that I have seen too many dogs end up at the vet suffering from collapsed windpipes because their owners did not know how to use the collars properly and jerked too vigorously on them. Choke chains were initially used only by trainers who understood that timing and an appropriate level of correction was important in making them work effectively. Despite the fact that choke chains have caused a number of deaths through misuse, they are still available to the general public without accompanying directions. If a dog is a serious puller, not even the discomfort of a crushed trachea will stop him from pulling. Unlike a regular collar, a choke chain is very dangerous if left on the dog without supervision, as the loops on either end can easily catch on something and the dog can strangle himself while trying to get free.

Prong or pinch collars

The prong or the pinch collar is supposed to be kinder than the choke chain because the pressure of the correction is more evenly distributed around the dog's neck. Do they hurt? They sure do. If you don't believe me, put one around your arm and give it a good yank. I do not like them either.

Martingales

The martingale is a double-loop design that tightens and loosens according to how tense the leash is. These are a good choice for dogs, such as Greyhounds, Whippets, and Borzois, whose heads are the same size or smaller than their necks. Martingale collars tighten enough around the neck to prevent the dog from slipping out, but don't tighten enough to choke. Wide collars are also good for these breeds.

Harnesses

Harnesses are much better for little dogs who have more delicate necks and who could otherwise really suffer if they were wearing a standard collar and then pulled on the leash. They fit around the body and distribute pressure evenly. However, some dogs pull harder when they are wearing a harness because they enjoy the reinforcing feeling of leaning against something. In that case, you can use a no-pull harness (see page 155).

How to introduce your puppy to a collar and leash

When you first bring your puppy home, he may never have experienced what it feels like to have a collar around his throat. He almost certainly will never have been walked on a leash before. These kinds of restraints will be alien and strange to him. The throat is a very vulnerable area on the dog's body. His instinct is to protect it. Many dogs also do not like the feeling of something going over their head. This is a very real invasion of their personal space.

Introduce your puppy to the collar first. Put it on for a few seconds. Try not to put it on over his head, but unbuckle it and do it up from the underside of the puppy's neck. Don't do it up too tightly; just let it sit loosely around his throat. Give him praise and rewards. Then take it off. Gradually build up the period of time you leave the collar on the puppy, using positive feedback, until he gets used to the sensation. Each time, tighten the collar a little more until it cannot slip over his head. Some dogs take longer to get used to collars than others. Once your dog is used to the collar, leave it on.

The next step is to introduce the leash. Clip it onto the puppy's collar and call his name. Praise and treat him when he comes to you. Practice putting the leash on and taking it off, rewarding calm behavior. This gets the puppy used to the idea of the leash. Always accustom a puppy to the collar and leash before you take him out of doors. Once he's outside, he will be bombarded by all kinds of new things. Don't let the collar and leash be part of that overwhelming experience. He'll have enough on his plate as it is.

How to teach your dog to walk on a leash

Teaching your dog to walk properly on a leash is a key part of dog training. If you do not teach him how to do it, he will pull and your daily walks with him will turn into constant struggles for control. For you, this may only mean that your arm is wrenched. The dog, however, could suffer serious damage to his throat. But if dogs pull, so do people. We've all seen people yanking puppies along on their leashes, while the poor creatures gasp and choke. Every time I see this, it makes my heart ache.

Begin training your puppy how to walk with you as soon as he is accustomed to his collar and leash. Practice around the house and out in the yard first, before taking him out in the street or to the park where there will be more distractions.

It's really important to begin this type of training as early as possible. For a start, it's easier to teach a puppy how to walk in the right way on the leash than it is to correct an older dog once he has been dragging you around for months. Secondly, puppies grow. If you own one of the larger breeds, by the time your dog's bad walking habits are well and truly established, he may be big enough to pull you over or drag you into traffic.

Some trainers advise owners to reinforce their status as top dog by always keeping in front when they are walking their dog. I don't agree with this practice. Dogs have four legs and we have two. Their pace is naturally much faster. Walking well on a leash is different from heeling. Before you can teach your dog to heel, you have to teach your dog to walk without pulling, to walk where you walk and not in a direction of his own choosing, and to stop when you stop.

The leash is like a telegraph wire. It transmits your feelings direct to the dog. If you are tense, the dog will feel it. Many people seize a leash and immediately tighten it up so the dog is tugged toward them. This gives a dog an immediate excuse to resist and something to pull against. Before long, you'll be battling for control, and communicating down the taut length of the leash just how annoyed and tense this makes you.

Here's what you should do:

Your aim is to get your dog to walk on a *relaxed* leash. So start out that way.

Clip the leash onto your puppy and walk with him around your home or in your yard. Give him praise and rewards as he is walking along. Puppies like to follow their owners, so he should be keen to move in the direction that you are moving.

As soon as he tugs on the leash or pulls, stop. Make like a tree. Be calm and wait for him to stop tugging.

When he does, when the leash is relaxed and he is looking up at you, praise him, give him a reward, and move off again.

Here's another way of doing it:

Another method you can try is to reverse direction. If he pulls, you simply turn and walk the other way. As you turn, lower your body slightly and motivate your dog to follow you by saying "let's go" in a high tone of voice. Praise him when he follows you.

Repeating this exercise will teach your puppy not to pull. It will also teach him that walking on a leash doesn't hurt, because as soon as he feels tightness on his throat, you stop or walk the other way. By not giving in to the pulling, you avoid reinforcing the behavior.

When you take your dog outside into the wide world, keep the training going. You can tighten the leash a little to motivate your dog to walk closer by your side when you cross a busy road. Always give him plenty of praise for walking well. Good dog behavior often goes unnoticed by owners. If your dog is doing what you want him to do, let him know how pleased you are.

Remember that every member of the family has to be consistent, and use the same commands when they are walking the dog.

Good dog behavior often goes unnoticed by owners.

Walkies!

Once dog-walking is part of your daily routine, your dog will look forward to this part of the day with huge anticipation. As the hour approaches, he will notice every single sign that a walk is imminent. Maybe you always get up, stretch, and put on your shoes beforehand. Maybe you put your keys in your pocket. Whatever you usually do in preparation for a walk, he'll have got the message before your hand even touches that leash or you utter that special word beginning with W.

The walk is one of the highlights of the dog's day, and he will express that in excited behavior. Some dogs run about in circles, some yap, some run back and forth to the door. In the wild, pack members display similar excited behavior before setting off on the hunt. It is thought that this limbers them up physically and reinforces their sense of pack identity.

Of course your dog is going to be excited when he knows he's about to go out. But you shouldn't let this become an issue of control.

Here's what you should do:

Your dog should sit before you put on the leash. Don't allow him to jump up. If he does, wait until you have his attention, ask him to sit again, and then put on the leash.

Once the leash is on, many dogs immediately pull in the direction of the door. Don't allow your dog to do this. If he pulls, stop. Wait until he is paying attention to you before moving on.

When you get to the door, ask your dog to sit. Then open the door a little. If your dog charges at it, shut it again. Repeat until you get to the point where you can open the door completely while the dog sits still.

Walk out of the door. If he pulls, stop and wait until the leash is relaxed again.

How to teach your dog to heel

Once your dog is walking well on a leash, you can teach him how to heel. Heeling is a refinement. When you're out walking your dog, you should not keep him walking to heel all of the time. But it is a very useful command when you are walking in crowded streets where there are many potential distractions or when your dog is off the leash in the park and you want to bring him back to walk by your side for whatever reason. Teach your dog to heel on the leash first, then teach him off the leash.

Here's how it works:

Choose the side you feel most comfortable having your dog. For me, it's the left.

Now imagine an invisible box attached to the left side of your leg.

Walk with your dog normally. When your dog comes into that box, as soon as his shoulders are by your left thigh, give him praise and a reward.

Then attach a sound and a signal to the action. As your dog comes into the box, slap your left thigh and say "heel."

When you change direction, slap your thigh and say "heel" just as you turn.

Here's a slightly different way of doing it:

Put your dog on the leash.

Then let your arm drop by your side, palm facing backward.

Your dog will naturally want to investigate. When he touches your palm with his nose, say "good boy" and treat. Repeat a few times.

Vary the exercise a little. Hold your hand out for a few seconds and remove it.

I sometimes use the command "touch." Or I might use no words at all. When your dog is touching your palm every time you put your hand down, add the command "heel" and pat your left (or right) leg.

If I am training very small dogs to heel, I sometimes use a target stick so I don't have to bend over so far. I wrap material around the bottom of the stick to bulk it out a little and make it easier for the dog to see. Instead of the dog touching my hand with his nose when he comes to heel, he touches the end of the target stick.

Letting your dog off the leash

Dogs need exercise, but they also deserve some freedom. Off the leash, your dog can explore the world at his own pace and in whichever direction his nose takes him. He may snuffle about, contentedly investigating every tantalizing whiff, or he may pick up a real turn of speed and run his socks off. Letting your dog off the leash gives him the chance to exercise aerobically. A good workout is a real stress-buster, and will make him much more content at home.

The "come" command has to be pretty solid before you can let your dog off the leash and expect him to come back to you reliably. See page 86 for how to teach it. Provided it is safe, you can let your puppy off the leash in the park and use the occasion as the opportunity to reinforce your teaching of the "come" command. Fenced-in areas within a park are good places for you to do this.

A good workout is a real stress-buster, and will make your dog much more content at home.

Out and about

Exercising your dog farther afield often involves a car journey. Try to get your dog accustomed to the car from a very early age if you are going to be driving around with him frequently. Use rewards and positive training to send the message that the car is a good place to be. Initially, introduce your puppy to the car when it is stationary. Feed your dog beside it or inside it. Play games with him and give him toys while he is sitting in it. Take him on short journeys before going longer distances.

Always use the proper means of restraint inside the car. You can put your dog in a harness, use a travel crate, or fit a grate. Whichever you choose, introduce him to the means of restraint gradually.

Never, ever leave a dog unattended in a car in warm weather. Dogs heat up very quickly and can easily die of heat exhaustion.

Exercise problems

Coming to grips with problems relating to exercising, particularly walking, is very important. If your dog does not walk properly on the leash, you won't enjoy taking him out, and neither will other members of your family. The result inevitably will be shorter and less frequent walks. That's not fair on your dog.

Problem: Pulling on the leash

This has got to be one of the most common dog-walking problems. It's so easy to teach a dog to walk properly, and it's a real pity when people don't. It may be a little time-consuming at first, but dogs who pull quickly get bored with all the stopping and changes of direction and once the lesson is learned, it's rarely forgotten.

If you have a persistent puller, you are going to have to take action. When we were making the pilot episode of *It's Me or the Dog*, we visited a family who owned an Old English Sheepdog named Blue. Old English Sheepdogs are big animals, and Blue had had next to no training on how to walk on a leash. He pulled. How he pulled! On one occasion he nearly pulled his owner into a busy road. Dogs that are as large as Blue and whose bad pulling habits are so ingrained need a different approach.

Solution: Using leaders and harnesses

I'm generally not in favor of using "quick-fix" equipment, but the no-pull harness is one of my favorite ways of curing a persistent pulling problem. Unlike normal harnesses, the leash is attached to the harness just behind the dog's neck, rather than at the back. Two straps, padded to prevent chafing, wrap around the legs. When the dog pulls forward, he feels as if he is being lifted off the ground, and so he stops.

I didn't use a harness on Blue, although they

do make them for dogs his size. Instead, I used a gentle leader. Gentle leaders work in the same way as a halter does on a horse. Once a horse is wearing a halter, it can be led around very easily because you have control of its head. The gentle leader consists of a nose loop that is designed to fit snugly, but not too tightly, around the muzzle, and a neck strap that attaches behind the ears at the top of the neck. The leash is attached to a loop under the chin or to a loop at the side. Instead of leading the dog by the neck, you lead him by his head. Wherever the head goes, the rest of the body will follow.

The gentle leader is not a muzzle. Your dog should be able to pant, bite, vomit, take treats, and drink water with it on. The noseband should not be too tight, or it could cause chafing and loss of hair around the nose. Never leave a leader on an unsupervised dog.

I use the gentle leader because it doesn't put any pressure on a dog's sensitive neck. There is no yanking involved. The dog simply cannot pull. As soon as the dog pulls forward, the head automatically comes to the side. However, when you are using the gentle leader, never jerk on it or make any other kind of leash correction. Jerking could hurt the dog's head.

Many dogs will struggle and resist as soon as a gentle leader is put on them because the feeling of pressure around the head and the muzzle is very different from the pressure of a collar. For that reason, it is important to desensitize your dog to the leader by making good things happen to him when you put it on.

I work for half a day putting a gentle leader on the dog and taking it off before I even venture out for a walk with the dog. Each time the leader goes on, the dog gets a delicious treat and lots of praise. After I have practiced putting the leader on and off, I attach a leash to it and walk the dog round the house for a minute or two, ignoring negative behavior and rewarding him when he's calm. Some dogs will try to remove the leader by pawing at their noses, shaking their heads, and rolling on the floor. Other dogs will find that the pressure immediately settles them down. That is because a mother dog will often take the muzzle of a puppy in her mouth as a calming reprimand, and the feeling of the leader is very similar.

While leaders are safe, they do have some drawbacks, which you must take into consideration. A leader can slip off the nose easily if the dog struggles enough, so it is best to keep a back-up leash attached to the normal collar until the dog stops struggling. It can also cause anxiety in some dogs. If your dog refuses to walk, pants excessively, urinates when you put the leader on, or exhibits any other sign of anxiety after a couple of days of use, then you'll have to look at another solution. Another type of leader is a Halti. It is similar to the gentle leader, but the noseband is not adjustable. Instead it fits more loosely around the muzzle.

In Blue's case, I was able to turn around two years' worth of pulling behavior in a short time using a gentle leader. Whenever he pulled, I reinforced the head-turning action of the leader by making a strong sound to motivate and distract him, followed by a "let's go" signal. And when he walked calmly next to me, I gave him plenty of praise.

Problem: Refusing to walk

You're taking your dog out for a walk. He seems excited at the prospect. You clip on his leash and out you go. You get a little way down the road and then he sits down. He won't budge. You coax him. Perhaps you give him a treat (wrong!). He gets up, walks a few more paces. Then he stops and plants his bottom on the ground again.

Solution: Regain control of the situation

Before you can sort this one out, you need to rule out any physical factors that might be causing the behavior. Most dogs love to go for walks. If your dog refuses to walk all of a sudden, he might be ill or in pain. The pavement may be too hot or too cold for his feet. Or there might be some other dog in the vicinity that is making him anxious and nervous.

Puppies are often very hesitant the first few times they go outside for a walk. You have to get them used to all the new sights and sounds very gradually. Never yank a puppy to his feet when he sits down. You've just added pain to the fear he's already experiencing.

If you are able to rule out all the above causes, you've got an issue of control on your hands. I found myself in this situation once with a Maltese. I went through all the scenarios, and came to the conclusion that the dog simply wanted to get her own way. What did I do? When she sat down, I turned my back on her and sat down, too. Right on the pavement. In the middle of Manhattan.

We sat there for an hour until the dog got bored and came up to me. I gave her lots of praise and we carried on from there.

Problem: Running off

Most of the time, when dogs run off and don't come back when they're called, it is a clear sign that the "come" command needs further work.

When your dog is running off out of sight, you may experience real anxiety. No one wants to lose their dog or see him run into danger.

Solution: It depends

If you are in a safe area and there is no way the dog can be harmed, the very worst thing you can do is run after him. This turns running away into a game of chase. Instead, make loud distracting noises, and as soon as he turns around to find out what all the fuss is about, lie down on the ground. Most of the time, the dog will come back to investigate. As soon as he does, praise him and reward him, no matter how anxious and upset he made you.

If you do have to run after your dog, try to keep up with him without him getting the idea that you are chasing him. Drop treats on the ground as you go. If he disappears from sight altogether, go back to the first treat and wait to see if his nose brings him back to you.

Problem: Chasing

All dogs are predisposed to chase. It's how they hunt in the wild. Some breeds, however, get more of a kick out of chasing than others. Chasing is a predatory instinct. In the domestic dog, however, it's more the thrill than the kill. Dogs will chase cats, birds, and squirrels without the first idea what they would do if they caught them.

If your dog is chasing a squirrel, you have to accept he will find it very difficult to obey your command to come back to you. What is more attractive to him at the moment, you or the squirrel? Sorry, but it's the squirrel.

Solution: Manage the environment

If you've got a bad squirrel- or cat-chaser on your hands, you're going to have to walk him on an extendable leash in the park. Otherwise, find a safe, enclosed area within the park and let him chase for a while to get it out of his system. This will release the stress that he is experiencing every time he sees a squirrel or cat and can't get at it.

Problem: Aggressive behavior on the leash

Your dog is a loving animal that wouldn't hurt a fly. He's friendly with other dogs in the park and gets along well with other people, too. Then one day you're walking him and he lunges out at another dog or person, seemingly with no warning. The next day he does it again. What's going on?

Solution: Distraction and conditioning

It is unrealistic to expect our dogs to be sociable with every dog or person they meet. After all, some strangers make you feel uneasy, don't they? In normal circumstances, when a dog encounters another dog that makes him feel scared, he will run away. But when he's on the leash, he can't do that. Instead, he might try an aggressive display to see if it scares the other dog off. If the "bad" dog goes away, your dog will think that his show of aggression has done the trick, and may be more likely to respond the same way next time.

If your dog repeatedly behaves this way, watch out for possible sources of trouble. If you see another dog coming your way, change direction or cross the street to put some distance between you. Use distraction to gain your dog's attention. Make a noise, ask him to sit and watch you. Do some obedience exercises with him to keep him focused on you. Once the other dog has passed and your dog has not shown any aggressive behavior, give him a fantastic treat. When you are getting good responses from your dog, you can gradually reduce the distance between him and other dogs.

Problem: Crazy in cars

There's a great place to walk your dog, but you have to drive to get there. The trouble is that every time you take your dog in the car, he barks himself senseless. You can't hear yourself think and you certainly can't concentrate on the road.

Solution: Find the cause and treat appropriately

Blue, the Old English Sheepdog who had such a problem with pulling on the leash, also went crazy in the car. As soon as Blue was put in the car, he started to bark. His constant barking was driving his owners crazy. The first thing I had to do was find out why he behaved the way that he did.

I asked the dog's owner to put Blue in the car. He did and Blue barked. Then I asked the owner to crouch down so that the dog could not see him and get into the car. Bent double and on all fours, the owner made his way to the front of the car. Blue, who had barked when he was first put in the car, fell silent. That is, until his owner got into the driving seat. Then the barking began again in earnest.

I then asked the owner to repeat the sequence, but this time get in on the passenger's side and scoot across. Silence from Blue.

What that told me was that Blue was barking out of habit and not anxiety. When he fell silent, it was because he could not see his owner. The usual sequence of events – Blue gets put into the car, Blue sees owner get into the driver's seat – had changed. The normal cues that triggered his barking response were missing. Like humans, dogs have rituals. When that ritual is a bad habit, it's up to you to vary the picture. In Blue's case, varying the picture meant he couldn't respond to the usual cues, and I was able to work on reinforcing his good behavior by rewarding him when he was calm.

If your dog goes crazy in cars, there could be many reasons:

He might associate the car with the walk at the end of it and be barking in excited anticipation. Break the habit by waiting for a while when you get to your destination before getting out of the car. That way the mere act of entering the car is disassociated in the dog's mind with the walk to come.

He might feel ill or uneasy in the car. Some dogs get carsick. Get him used to car journeys gradually, when he is a puppy, and use a proper harness or restraint to stop him from being thrown around when the car brakes or turns.

He might be chasing what he can see out of the window. Cars go fast. What the dog sees out of the window, however, are objects moving fast. Keep him in a travel crate where he cannot be distracted by the view.

Ain't Misbehaving
teach your dog how to live in your world

Many people assume that because a dog is a social animal, he already has the skills he needs to live happily alongside humans. That is not the case. A dog's social skills, which he picks up from his mother and littermates, are designed to help him live in a dog pack. Once he has left his littermates behind, he needs to learn how to live with you in your home.

Our family pets are the result of centuries and centuries of domestication. However, when you bring a new puppy home, or even an adult dog, that does not mean he will automatically recognize your home as a familiar, comfortable place where he would like to be. It's up to you to show him that he can be relaxed and confident in his new surroundings.

How do you do that? One of the ways is by creating a positive environment in which his needs for affection and stimulation can be met. Obedience training provides a good framework for this. But obedience training, on its own, is not enough. You also need to introduce your new family member to other people, children and other dogs, as well as to the sounds, sights, smells, textures, and different locations that make up his new world. You have to make it easy for him to do well.

Settling a new puppy

One minute your puppy is playing with his littermates and sleeping curled up beside them, and the next, those littermates are nowhere to be seen and he's sleeping by himself in a new place, a place his senses tell him is very different from everything he has ever known. Many puppies settle quickly into their new homes. Others take a little longer. But even confident, outgoing puppies find the first few nights a little difficult.

I always let a new puppy sleep in the same room as me for the first week or so. Once he has settled a little, I move his bed or night crate outside into the hall. A week or so later, he's usually happy enough to sleep on his own in the kitchen.

Be careful not to overtire your puppy in the early weeks. Puppies, like small children, need plenty of naps because they are still developing and growing. At the same time, your puppy will be taking in vast amounts of new information about his new home, and mental work can be more exhausting than physical activity.

It is not unusual for dog breeders to live in rural areas. If you have bought your dog from a breeder who lives in a quiet, remote location and you live in the suburbs or the city, think about what a difference that makes to your dog. He's spent the first weeks of his life seeing only a few people every day and hearing only a few cars go past. That's all he knows. Now, all of a sudden, he's in a much busier, noisier environment. It's up to you to introduce him to his new surroundings in a controlled way so that he learns to live in his new world with confidence.

Making the introductions

Little puppies are naturally very inquisitive and greet new experiences and other creatures in an open, friendly way. Like babies and small children, they're programmed to explore the world around them. If they were too fearful to do that, they would never learn. Play-fighting with littermates or practicing their bite to learn its strength are just a couple of ways in which they pick up the kind of information that will help them read signs and signals in later life.

When a puppy reaches about 16 weeks, however, something happens to that irrepressible curiosity. In the wild, this is the age when a puppy's mother would begin to push him away and encourage him to fend for himself. A puppy that remained friendly, open, and curious in those circumstances probably would not survive for long. After 16 weeks, puppies greet new things much more cautiously, even fearfully. They are suspicious of what they have not encountered before. When a puppy is very young, he sees each new experience as potentially good and pleasurable until persuaded otherwise by his experience. After 16 weeks, the opposite is the case.

This means you have a relatively small window of opportunity to introduce your puppy to his new world. Of course, you can introduce puppies over 16 weeks to new things. You should, and, as circumstances change, you will have to. But you stand a much better chance of avoiding problems in the future if you have already exposed him, in a controlled way, to as many new situations and experiences in the early weeks as possible, while his natural curiosity is still strong. Past this critical period, you will be going against the flow.

This process of introduction is known as socialization. You are doing your puppy no favors if you isolate him from the world in the early weeks after you bring him home. Even if you are giving him plenty of attention, he still needs to meet new situations. That does not mean you should overload him with different sensations and experiences, but it does mean you need to show him the kind of things he will be encountering on a regular basis simply by virtue of living in your human world.

What kind of things should you introduce to your puppy?

Your touch

Dogs are affectionate creatures, but they need to learn that when you touch them, you are not a threat. Dogs that have been mistreated in their early months remain fearful of human handling because they have learned the opposite.

Other people, including children

A puppy will quickly learn to recognize his new human pack. He'll learn their scent and the sound of their voices. But he also needs to learn that visitors to your home or strangers that he encounters outside it are not sources of threat.

Other dogs

Up until he leaves his litter, your puppy's experience of other dogs will most probably have been limited to his immediate family. Once he is fully protected by his vaccinations, you need to take him out into situations where he can interact with other dogs.

Essential equipment, such as the collar, leash, and grooming tools

Introduce him to them gradually.

Locations

Introduce your dog to as many different locations as possible, starting with different rooms in the home, moving out into the yard and from there to the street and the park. Don't just go to the same park. Vary your destinations and the routes you take to get there.

The car

Many owners do little to prepare their dog for traveling in a car, and yet expect them to behave the first time they are driven anywhere.

The vet's

I give many talks at vets' offices, and I always encourage owners to bring their puppies with them and get them used to the sights and smells of a clinic. The puppies get fed treats and are allowed to play and so they associate being at the vet's with good things.

While you shouldn't bombard your dog with too many new experiences at once, make sure his early weeks with you contain plenty of variety. Use food treats and toys to teach your dog to associate these new experiences with pleasure. He will begin to get the message that good things happen when children are around, for example, or when he is in the car.

Observe your dog when he meets new experiences and note his reactions. Ignore negative behavior and reward a calm response. It sounds like common sense, doesn't it? But many people do exactly the opposite.

Let's take a simple example. You're out walking your puppy and a fire engine goes past, sirens blaring. He cowers and barks. You rush to comfort the dog, petting him and telling him, "Poor puppy. Did the sound hurt your ears? It's all right. It's just a fire engine."

Think about that for a minute. Now remember, the puppy doesn't understand English. You could explain to a child all about fire engines and why they need to make a lot of noise and that would help the child get over his fear. But the dog doesn't understand the meaning of the words that you've said. What he does understand is that you rewarded him for cowering and barking. That reward came in the form of your attention and your soft tone of voice. The next time a fire engine goes past, he will be more inclined to behave the same way he did the first time. What you should have done was ignore the behavior. Be there as your dog's protector, but don't reinforce nervous behavior.

Let's imagine a different scenario. You're out walking your puppy and a fire engine goes past, sirens blaring. Your puppy doesn't turn a hair. Instead, he's still happily trotting along beside you. You think nothing of it and carry on to the park. What you should have done was reward your dog's calm behavior.

When puppies meet new situations and react calmly, many owners don't notice the behavior at all. Why is that? Always reward the behavior you want to encourage. That way you will give your dog confidence because he will gain a clear understanding of how you expect him to behave.

Each dog is an individual. Breeds, however, tend to share certain characteristics. Border Collies, bred to respond to whistles and vocal signals while herding, are very sensitive to sound, and may find a noisy environment or sudden noises more distressing than other types of dogs. Guarding breeds, such as German Shepherds, may be more protective around strangers and other dogs. Whatever traits your dog displays, this period of socialization is a learning process on both sides. You need to build up a picture of the way your dog responds in different situations so that you can manage his environment in an appropriate way.

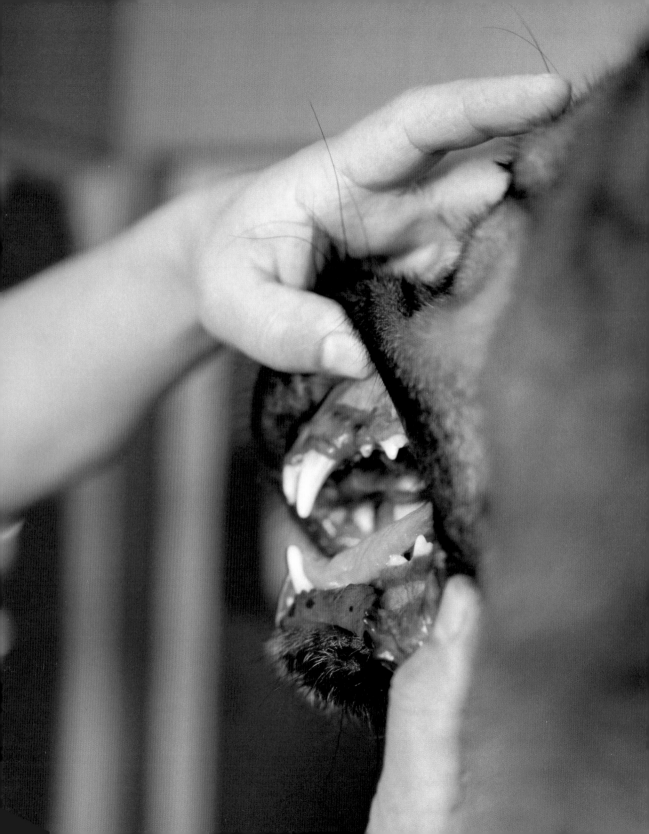

Handling your dog

Getting a dog used to your touch is very important. It builds up a bond of affection between you and your pet, but it also enables you to handle him safely in situations such as check-ups at the vet's, where different parts of his body will be prodded and poked.

Most people need no encouragement to cuddle and stroke their puppy. Bear in mind, however, that this type of touching is not in the dog's repertoire of natural behaviors. Although a dog will use his paw on occasion, he is more likely to put something into his mouth to explore it and find out what it's like. He may nuzzle you affectionately, or find it comforting to sit or lie so that his body is in contact with yours, but that's very different from instinctively finding stroking and petting a welcome sensation.

Grooming provides an opportunity to introduce your dog to your touch. So does massage. Just like humans, dogs find massage very calming and relaxing. You can press your thumbs on either side of his spine and make gentle, circling motions all the way down. You can stroke his ears. If you are very careful, you can massage the skin between his foot pads.

Teaching your dog to be independent

A dog is utterly dependent on his human pack for all the essentials of life: food, shelter, exercise, company, stimulation, and protection from danger. That's no reason, however, to treat him like a baby. People who baby their dogs wind up with pets that are overly attached, insecure, and anxious. Your dog follows you everywhere you go. You see this as proof of devotion. It's not. He just cannot cope with being away from you.

Your puppy will naturally tend to follow you around. It's not surprising. You are the source of all the good things in his life. Once he has settled in to his new home, however, you should begin to encourage him to be a little more independent. That does not mean he will need you any less, it just means that he will not rely on you so completely for his emotional security.

An independent dog is not a dog that does what he likes, whenever he wants. Instead, he's confident enough in himself to allow you to disappear for periods of time. He won't trail around after you all the time or get upset if you close the bathroom door.

Here are some ways to encourage independence:

Don't always respond immediately to his demands for attention. Give him attention on your terms. If he comes to sit by you, move away. If he paws at you and whines, ignore him. This is not cruel or rejecting on your part. This is simply a way of providing him with an all-important social skill.

If he is overly boisterous when he greets you after an absence, ignore him until he has calmed down and then reward him for calm behavior. If he jumps up, turn around.

Make him work for attention by doing some obedience training with him.

Keep him stimulated with play and exercise.

Don't allow him to follow you whenever he wants and wherever he wants. Close the door behind you.

When you go out

A dog that is overly attached to his owner will find periods of separation very difficult. He has no way of knowing how long you will be gone, or whether you will ever come back. Teaching your dog to be more independent will help him cope with any period of absence in a much more confident way.

Here's what you should do:

You will make things much worse for the dog if you make a big fuss when you leave. Don't say: "See you later. I won't be long, I promise!" while fondling your dog's ears. Instead, keep it low-key, withdrawing your attention from your dog 20 minutes before you leave. Keep it low-key when you return. Don't say: "Oh! Did you miss me?" as he jumps all over you. Instead, show him that your return is no big deal. You were out, and now you're back.

Leave him in a dog-proofed area with toys and other things to keep him busy. Cubes that you can stuff with treats will keep him occupied for quite a while (see page 208).

Dogs are very sensitive to changes in their environment. So what usually happens when you go out? Do you turn off the radio and the TV? Do you turn out the lights? If you do, your dog will find that his immediate world has suddenly changed from one that was bright and full of comforting sounds to a silent, dark place. Plus, you're gone.

Here, you can do a great deal to ease the stress of your absence by managing the dog's environment. Keep the lights on when you go out. Leave the radio or the TV on. I often set the TV to a news channel so that the dog can hear voices. Or I'll leave music playing. Any piece of music that is repetitive and not overly dynamic works well. I play Mozart, Bach, and Celtic music to my dogs.

Make sure you are not gone too long. Four to six hours is the most you should leave an adult dog on his own.

Adolescence

Yes, dogs, too, have their teenage years (thankfully measured in months, not years). Around the age of six months, just when you are congratulating yourself that your new family member has settled in nicely, is fully house-trained, and has stopped chewing everything in sight, he will suddenly start to show signs that he is developing a mind of his own.

Up till now, he's been a good boy and has always come when you called him. Now, however, he's straying a little further away in the park and taking his own sweet time to return.

Between 6 and 18 months, before your dog is fully adult, you need to step up training, exercise, and stimulation. The behavior that is sometimes seen in adolescent dogs is not a sign that the dog has forgotten what he has been taught, or that he is only now showing his true colors. It's just another learning stage, as adolescence is in humans. Keep your teenage dog active and stimulated, and encourage his independence through training, and you will be rewarded with a mature, confident dog before too long.

Make sure you neuter your pet before the sex hormones have a chance to affect his behavior. Neutering can help calm an adolescent dog (see page 36).

Everyone loves puppies, whether they treat them properly or not. But many dogs that find themselves in shelters are adolescents whose owners have found that their sweet, cuddly little puppy has suddenly grown bigger and harder to handle. Dogs are not disposable property, or problems that we can hand over to someone else to sort out when we aren't prepared to invest the time to raise them properly. They deserve our best shot.

Children and dogs

According to the Humane Society of the United States, 50% of children will be bitten by a dog before their 12th birthday, with highest incidences occurring in children under five. Most dog bites go unreported, so the figures could well be much higher. In Britain, an average of 200,000 dog bites are reported each year. One third to a half of these are suffered by children, often to the face.

Only a small percentage of these bites require medical treatment, but most come from a dog that the child knows, either the family pet or a friend's dog. These statistics indicate that we have much more work to do teaching children how to behave around dogs – and, of course, vice versa.

A dog bite can be serious and traumatic, especially for children. Being bitten by a dog can make a child distrust not only the dog that bit them, but also all dogs that they will ever meet in the course of their lives. It's up to you as a parent to ensure that your child knows what to do and how to behave around dogs.

Children are particularly at risk for dog bites for several reasons. They move fast, and speed provokes a dog's chasing instincts. Their voices are high, and high voices are not only less authoritative, they also excite dogs and scare them. Added to which, children are small. They are closer to a dog's eye level and to the floor, which is a dog's feeding level. A child will often tease a dog with food, or explore his body by pulling his tail.

Rules for parents:

Never give in to a child who begs you for a dog, unless you are prepared to look after the dog yourself. You will be the primary caregiver, whether it is your child's dog or not. Over the age of six, your children will be mature enough to share some of the responsibility, and owning a pet will teach them many things, including how to care for an animal and treat him with respect. But don't fool yourself. You'll be doing most of the work.

Choose a dog or a breed that is appropriate for your family. If you want an easygoing family pet, for example, don't get a Terrier.

Never leave a young child alone with a dog.

Teach your children the right way to pet a dog (see page 179).

Teach your children how to spot the signs that a dog might bite. These include: ears back and flattened, lips parted, staring eyes with big pupils, bared teeth or quivering lips, hackles raised on the back, tense and frozen body, tail that is not wagging or is moving slowly. Tell your children not to approach any dog that is showing those signs.

Teach your children to treat dogs nicely and with respect, the way they would like to be treated themselves.

Train your puppy to be calm around children. Teach your puppy bite-inhibition if he has a tendency to nip. Spay and neuter your dog.

Rules to teach your children:

Never touch a dog you do not know.

If you do know the dog, ask permission from the owner first.

Even when you have permission, don't invade the dog's body space. Allow the dog to come up to you and sniff the top of your hand. If he doesn't want to come and greet you, leave him alone.

Don't approach a dog from behind. Don't pet a dog directly on the top of its head. It could be threatening. Rub him on his chest instead.

Never stare at a dog and never put your face close to a dog's face. When you greet a dog, look at him briefly and then look away. Look at him again and look away. These calming signals are very important because they show the dog that you are not a threat.

Do not tease a dog with food or toys.

Do not go up to a dog that has been tied up or left at the end of a chain in the garden.

Tell an adult immediately if you see a dog loose in your neighborhood. Do not touch him.

Do not touch a dog while he is eating.

Do not touch a dog while he is sleeping. You might startle or scare him, and he could react without thinking and snap at you.

Don't scream and run away from a dog. If a dog comes up to you and you are scared, stand still, look away from him, and walk off slowly with your arms folded.

Remember that your dog is an animal and not a cuddly toy. Some dogs don't like being hugged. Be gentle with your dog. Don't play rough with him.

New baby in the family

I have advised parents-to-be for many years how to prepare their dogs for the arrival of a new baby. It wasn't until the birth of my daughter, Alexandra ,that I had the opportunity to put my advice into practice, and to show my animals that the little bundle in my arms was a wonderful addition to our family. As a dog trainer and behavior counselor, I thought I had all the answers. As a mother, I discovered that much more was needed to be done to help my dogs feel comfortable around my daughter and to help me cope with the overwhelming responsibility of being a new mom. So, for pregnant pet-owners and fathers-to-be, here is the ultimate guide to baby-proofing your dog.

Baby-proofing your dog is all about making your dog feel comfortable and safe with the new changes that your baby will bring to family life. Some dogs have never seen a baby, let alone lived with one in the same house. How does your dog react around other babies who cry loudly? What does he do when a child runs past? Does he get over-excited, or remain calm? Does his body tense when a child comes too near, or is he eager to greet them? Observing your dog's reactions around other children will give you an indication of what you can expect when your baby arrives.

We all know that a dog's sense of smell is immensely superior to ours. A dog is able to detect the smell of human perspiration at a concentration up to a million times lower than humans can detect. Your baby is going to smell fascinating to your dog, so introduce him now to baby smells. Allow him to explore the sweet-smelling baby products that you will be using. When your baby is born, have a friend or family member bring home a blanket that your baby has been wrapped in. Allow the dog to smell the blanket and ask that friend or family member to praise him as he sniffs it, give him a delicious treat, and allow him to smell again. This should be repeated a number of times until the baby comes home.

The cry of a newborn makes a new mom anxious. It can also affect your dog. Before the big day, introduce your dog to baby sounds. All my mothers-to-be receive a 15-minute tape of a crying baby, which they play three to four times a day for a week at a low setting so that the dog can hardly hear it. Good things such as play, petting, and treats happen while the tape is playing. If the dog

seems comfortable, the volume is gradually increased until it is very loud. If the dog becomes stressed at any time, the volume is decreased to the previous comfort level for a couple of days, until the dog is relaxed, and then the process is continued. You can try the same thing yourself. While a tape can't reproduce the unique cry of your baby, over a period of weeks before your baby is born, your dog will become used to a sound he will soon be hearing very often.

Show your dog what a baby looks and feels like. Buy a life-sized baby doll and allow your dog to touch the doll's feet with his nose. Praise and treat. Wrap the doll in a blanket and walk around with the doll in your arms. Sit with the doll in one arm, as if you are feeding it, and stroke your dog with your other hand. Your dog will begin to associate the close presence of your baby with good things happening to him. Use food treats to reward your dog for calm behavior, or you can give him his favorite toy or play his favorite game with him while holding the doll.

Walking your dog helps you stay fit throughout your pregnancy. At this stage, however, your dog needs to learn how to walk with a stroller. If your dog pulls on the leash, get another person to walk him while you push the stroller. Hire a private trainer or take your dog to a training class so that he can learn to walk alongside the stroller. The more you practice now the easier it will be.

If you have never done any obedience training with your dog and have poor control over him, enroll him in a training class or hire a private in-home trainer to work with you. A dog who responds well to commands and who understands that jumping up on you when you have a baby in your arms is unacceptable will be much easier to live with when the baby arrives.

Have a plan ready a few months before delivery, so that your dog has somewhere to go when you are admitted to the hospital. When you come home, allow a family member to carry your baby into the house while you spend time greeting the dog. After the greeting is over, sit down on the sofa with the baby in your arms and introduce your dog to the new member of the family. Keep your body relaxed throughout the introductions, and praise your dog for good behavior. From the time you bring your baby home until your child is at least six to eight years of age, he or she should never be left unsupervised with any dog, no matter how well-mannered and well-trained that dog might be.

New dog in the family

Many of my clients come to see me when they encounter problems settling a new dog into a family that already includes another dog – or two or three.

Let's keep it simple for the moment. You already have a dog and would like to get another one. What can you expect? And how can you settle the new dog into the family and keep both of your dogs happy?

Dogs make good companions for each other. But you can't just go out and get another dog, and leave the two of them to get on with it. Your new dog will need just as much training and attention as the one you already have. A second dog is not the solution if your dog is bored and isolated. On the other hand, sometimes an older dog will provide so much fun and stimulation for a younger one that the young dog will not look to you to meet those needs, and will be harder to train as a consequence.

Many people decide to get a new dog when the dog they already own is getting on in years. Sometimes the presence of a puppy or younger dog will give an old dog a new lease on life and a fresh source of stimulation. But the cavortings of a puppy can also put a strain on an old dog, which has very much lower levels of activity. Remember that different breeds vary in their need for exercise. It's best if your new dog has similar energy levels to those of the dog you already have.

At the same time, make sure that your new puppy comes from a good home and has been properly socialized. A puppy that has not had the right kind of formative experiences will not be able to read the signals that your dog is giving, which may lead to fights.

All dogs are individuals, and it isn't always possible to predict how two animals will get on, even those of the same breed. You can do a lot to make the process easier, but you can't always guarantee that things will turn out all right. Dogs don't get to choose their new friends or companions, and sometimes it just doesn't work out. Some breeds find it harder to share their humans with other dogs. And if your dog has already shown that he has problems with other dogs, don't think about getting another one. Bringing the source of the problem into your home is not going to mend your pet's ways.

Settling him in

Introduce the new arrival in a calm and controlled way. Puppies are cute, and everyone likes to give them lots of attention. They also demand more of your attention because they require more frequent feeding and need to be taken out more often. Don't go overboard when the new puppy arrives. Show your dog that he is still important to you and has not been supplanted by the new arrival. As far as possible, treat both dogs equally. Praise and reward your older dog when he is calm around the puppy.

Dogs can be very protective of their resources. These include food, toys, territory, and human attention. Manage your environment so that both dogs have less opportunity to compete over these resources. Give each dog time with you by himself. Keep control of the dogs' toys, and use them as rewards in training sessions or in individual playtimes. Reward your older dog with a jackpot treat when he behaves well around the new arrival, and pay him slightly less attention when the puppy is out of the room. This will teach him that good things happen around the puppy, and that the puppy is a source of fun and pleasure.

Social problems

Genetics and breeding account for a small percentage of social problems in dogs. Most of the time, a problem such as excessive barking or fear of the vet can be attributed to one or two causes.

One of the most common causes of behavioral problems in dogs is isolation. Dogs aren't meant to live on their own any more than we are. When a dog is left alone for too long, he suffers from a range of negative emotions: boredom, frustration, anxiety, and sheer misery.

The other common cause of behavioral problems is poor socialization. Puppies who are not introduced early enough to new experiences tend to meet new situations with fear and lack of confidence in later life.

It's always better to prevent problems from arising by handling and looking after your dog properly from day one. The more often a dog rehearses his bad behavior, the more ingrained the habit becomes. Many problems can be turned around, however. You just need patience and time.

Remember that most dog problems have nothing to do with dogs. They're people problems.

Problem: The backyard barker

Your dog barks incessantly in the yard. Your neighbors are complaining. You try to tell your dog to be quiet, but he just won't stop yapping away. He's a real noise nuisance, and one day you worry he's going to be reported.

Solution: Identify the cause and treat appropriately

Barking is an essential form of dog communication. Isolated episodes of barking are often simply the result of the dog barking in response to something he's seen – a squirrel, a bird, another dog. Excessive barking is a different matter. The first thing you have to do is work out why your dog is barking so much.

Most backyard barkers are not getting the stimulation and exercise they need. Instead of the dog getting a decent walk, he's being left out in the yard to amuse himself. He's bored and isolated. The solution here is obvious. The dog needs more fun and attention in his life – long walks, agility classes, and plenty of company.

Sometimes dogs get into the habit of barking because their owners reward them for doing so. Your dog barks in the yard, you chase him, or you bribe him with a treat to come indoors. A good game of chase and a treat? Of course the dog's going to do it again.

Here's what you should do:

- When your dog barks, don't tell him to be quiet. It might sound like you are joining in. Make a distracting noise and then wait for your dog's attention.

- If he gives you his attention and is quiet, reward him.

- If your dog barks at you for attention, turn your back and don't give him any attention. Wait for him to stop.

- When he's quiet, reward the silence with your attention.

- Reward the quiet. Don't reward the barking.

I once advised an owner whose two Shelties were barking so much his neighbor was up in arms. The owner lived in a big house by a golf course where he liked to walk his dogs. Getting to the golf course meant he had to take his dogs through his yard and out through a gate at the bottom. From the time the dogs saw their owner reach for the leashes until they got to the golf course, the dogs barked their heads off. Shelties have a tendency to bark anyway, but these dogs really went for it.

What I did was break the entire "going out for a walk" sequence down into small steps. We started with the owner sitting in a chair. Then I asked him to get up as if he was going to get the dogs' leashes. The dogs barked, so I asked the owner to sit down again. The dogs fell silent. We repeated this over and over until the owner was able to get up and go for the leashes while the dogs remained silent.

Each trigger point in the entire sequence was treated in the same way. Putting on the leashes. Reaching a hand out to the door. Opening the door. Walking out of the door into the yard. Walking halfway down the yard. Reaching the gate. Opening the gate.

At every stage, if the dogs barked, they were immediately taken back into the house and the whole process was started all over again. All in all, it took an hour before the Shelties made it to the gate without barking. An hour is not very long to break a bad habit like this. The strategy worked because the bad behavior was not being reinforced with any attention. The dogs were only rewarded with a walk when they were quiet.

Barking collars

The barking or citronella collar is another of those quick-fix solutions we humans like so much. It's a collar with a box attached to it that sits under the dog's jaw. The action of barking depresses the box and sends a citrus spray right up the dog's nose. Of course, as if by a miracle, the dog will stop barking. The citrus spray is vile to him. But the barking collar is not a solution to the problem; it is a means of control. Dogs find them very stressful. Wouldn't you find it stressful if you weren't allowed to speak?

In all my time as a trainer, I have used a barking collar only once, and that was in a very extreme circumstance. Barking dogs in apartments are a real problem in Manhattan. When my client called me, he had just been served with an eviction notice because his two Dachshunds were barking in his apartment all day long. I used the collar for a single day while efforts went on to overrule the eviction. Meanwhile, I found a dog-walker who could take the dogs to a doggy daycare center while the owner was at work. The next day, the dogs had a brand-new lifestyle. With more stimulation and company, they were no longer bored and isolated, which had been causing the barking in the first place.

This is a prime example of an owner not providing enough stimulation for his dogs. Despite the fact that he was out all day, every day, he was angry at his dogs and blamed them for the fact that he had been served an eviction notice. I quickly made him see that he was the one who had caused his dogs' behavior. I didn't want to use the barking collar, but I also didn't want those beautiful dogs to end up in a shelter.

Problem: Jumping up on people

Every time you come into the room, your dog rushes over to greet you and jumps up on you. You don't mind very much – after all, your dog is just pleased to see you. But the other day he greeted your friend the same way, and your friend doesn't like dogs. Perhaps the answer is to meet your friend somewhere else in the future.

Solution: No attention

You need to teach your dog from the word go that jumping up on people is unacceptable. You may tell yourself that you don't mind it, but is that really true? What about when you're wearing your best clothes and you're just about to go out, and then your dog jumps up and his claws snag your best skirt or his paws leave muddy prints on your trousers? You don't like it then, do you? Dogs have no gray areas. You can't teach a dog that jumping up is sometimes OK and sometimes not.

It's not just about good doggy manners or saving on the dry cleaning bill. If your dog goes nuts in his greeting behavior every time someone comes to your house, you may find yourself avoiding such situations simply out of embarrassment. And while it's one thing for your Spaniel to hurl himself at you, if he did the same to a small child, he could hurt or scare that child very badly.

The solution is to give your dog no attention for jumping up or for any other crazy greeting behavior. None whatsoever. Turn away and don't look at him, talk to him, or touch him. Wait until he has calmed himself down, and gotten four paws on the ground, then reward the calm behavior.

Problem: Barking at strangers

Your dog barks at everyone who comes to the door. You haven't had any mail in days and you're beginning to suspect that the mailman has been skipping your house.

Solution: Teach the dog that strangers are a good thing

Think about it from the dog's point of view. The mailman comes up to the door. The dog barks. The mailman retreats. In the dog's mind, it was the barking that made the mailman go away. The next time the mailman comes, the dog will do it again.

Dogs bark at strangers for a variety of reasons. They may be defending their territory or protecting their resources (one of which is you). They may be anxious or nervous.

The answer is to teach your dog that strangers can be good things. This is a technique called "desensitization," and it can be used to modify many types of unwanted behavior. See the next page for how it works.

Here's what you should do:

Don't allow your dog to greet anyone at the door.

Put a bowl of chicken treats beside the door or hang a bag of treats over the door handle.

When guests come to your home, tell them to ignore the dog while you work with him doing some obedience exercises. Reward him with a piece of chicken.

Tell your guests to throw some chicken to your dog, but not to look at him.

Don't encourage other contact between your guests and your dog until he is used to their presence.

If your dog goes up to a guest, ask the guest to give your dog a treat without making eye contact. The more relaxed the guest can be, the better.

If the dog is relaxed and makes an effort to interact with your guest, you can then allow your guest to respond to this in a calm manner.

If your dog starts to behave badly again, say "ah" loudly and remove him from the room.

After a few minutes, let him come back in again.

Dogs catch on to this one pretty fast. Guests mean chicken!

Problem: Separation anxiety

You can't leave your dog alone for a minute. He howls when you take a bath. He chews up his basket when you leave the house. Now he's having little accidents.

Solution: Independence training and working on the cues

How long it takes to turn this problem around depends on the severity of the dog's anxiety. If he's mildly upset, you can sort it out pretty quickly. More serious cases take time.

In mild cases:

- Follow the advice given for independence training on page 170.

- The dog feels the separation anxiety most intensely at the moment of departure, so distance yourself from him and pay him less attention 20 minutes beforehand.

- Manage his environment. Make sure he has enough exercise. Exercise is good for stress in animals and a tired dog is less likely to get upset. Give him a good workout before you leave.

- Arrange for a dog-walker or dog-sitter to come in if you need to be out regularly.

Usually when you are trying to change a dog's behavior, you set things up so that the dog can't rehearse his bad habits. With separation anxiety, it's not that easy because you can't stay with the dog for every minute of the day, week in, week out.

A bad case:

I once advised a Labrador owner who was at her wit's end. The dog had one of the worst cases of separation anxiety I have ever seen. Every time the woman got ready to go out, the dog went crazy. When she did go out, he would try to eat through the wall. But he was a beloved pet, and she was desperate for a solution.

Dogs are no fools, and we are creatures of habit. That makes it easy for them to pick up the signals that tell them when we are about to leave the house. You do your makeup. You get your keys. You find your handbag.

We worked at desensitizing this dog to every cue he was picking up from his owner. So she put her clothes on and then took them off again lots of times during the day. Each time the dog expected her to leave, but she didn't. She put on her makeup and stayed in the house. She brushed her teeth, she went away to do something else, then she pretended to brush her teeth again. She put her handbag into a garbage bag and took it out of the house. Then she came back in. The next time, she put her handbag into a shopping bag, and took it out of the house. Then she came back in again.

We built up the time she was out of the house gradually from 30 seconds, to a minute, to three minutes. After two weeks, she was able to leave the house for 10 minutes. (I told you it was a serious case.)

At the same time, I got the owner to spray a light perfume on the door as she was about to come into the room where she had left the dog. Each time she came back, she sprayed the perfume and walked through the door. In time, the dog recognized that the perfume meant she was about to come back. And that meant she could spray the perfume before she went out. The lingering scent then served as a reassurance to the dog.

This entire process of desensitization took six weeks. To the owner, who was desperate to keep her dog, it was well worth it.

Problem: Your dog is jealous of the new love in your life

Your single days are over, and you've met the love of your life. The trouble is that your dog doesn't seem to feel the way you do, and he's making that perfectly plain. Then one day your partner says the words you have been dreading: "It's me or the dog." What do you do?

Solution: Teach your dog that your new partner is a good thing

One of my clients owned a Weimaraner that became very upset when the man got a new girlfriend. The dog would bark and lunge at the girlfriend whenever the couple cuddled and kissed. He tried to nip the girlfriend whenever his owner showed her any affection or attention. Then he peed on the girlfriend's coat.

Are dogs jealous of humans? I don't know. They can certainly react badly when they sense they are not getting the attention that they want from their owners. Peeing on clothing that belongs to the "rival" is not a conscious attempt on the dog's part to do something bad. It's sending out a message: "I'm putting my scent over your scent. I belong here."

We worked on showing the dog that the girlfriend was a good thing. I hung a bag of chicken outside the door to the room and each time the woman entered, she would throw a piece of chicken at the dog, avoiding eye contact. When the man put his hand out to touch the woman, he would pet and feed the dog with the other. The woman fed the dog, too. Gradually, I managed to get the couple as close on the sofa as they wanted to be without the dog reacting badly.

Problem: Biting in a puppy

Your puppy chews everything, including your hand. Sometimes he really nips you. Will he grow out of it, or is he more likely to bite someone in future?

Solution: Mouthing and biting stops play

It is really important right away to distinguish between normal puppy "mouthing" and a bite. Many people think that mouthing is the same thing as biting. It isn't. Mouthing is how puppies explore their environment; it tells them the shape and texture of things. Puppies and dogs will also mouth each other during play. While mouthing is perfectly normal, it has to be discouraged while the dog is still young so that the puppy doesn't grow up to think that it's OK to have a good chew on your arm with his adult teeth.

A puppy that mouths too much may not have remained with his littermates long enough to learn bite-inhibition. Or he's just over-exuberant. If that's the case, you'll have to teach him that chewing on you hurts!

Here's what you should do:

Let your puppy play and chew on toys, but as soon as he chews on you say a short, sharp "ouch," or give a yelp: "iiee!" A yelp is the type of feedback he would get from another dog.

If he continues, say "ouch" again, and leave the room or ignore him for a moment.

Return and resume play.

Repeat until he develops a softer mouth. Biting stops play.

Problem: Biting in an adult dog

Your dog has committed the ultimate canine crime and bitten someone. Does this mean you will have to have him put down?

Solution: Modify the dog's behavior

The first thing to establish is whether it was a bite at all. If you did not see the incident, you need to have a look at the injury. If there is no sign of damage, but the person still reports a bite, it's not a bite, it's a snap. And that's something different.

What is a dog bite? You might think that's a strange question. But a puppy or dog that understands his bite strength – that is to say, who has an "inhibited" bite – will very rarely bite another member of his human pack unless severely provoked or in pain. He may snap or attempt to nip, but he will not sink his teeth in and cause a wound that punctures the skin. If your dog snaps and doesn't bite you, it's not because he missed. It's because he didn't intend to bite you, he intended to warn you. A dog bite is a puncture wound that actually breaks the skin.

When humans lash out physically, we hit. Dogs use their mouths and bite. Biting in an adult dog is serious behavior and one that tends to get a dog labelled as aggressive, dominant, or territorial, and many worse things besides.

When a dog bites, people tend to think either that the animal is just plain bad by nature, or that he is trying to exert his authority through aggression. I see something rather different. I see a supremely insecure dog that is trying to get some control of the situation he is in. Aggression is important for a dog's survival in the wild. Without that instinct, he would be killed and eaten. Some degree of aggression is normal

in dogs. It is a product of fear – the dog feels that he must protect himself from threat.

To sort out this problem, you need to find out why the dog is behaving this way. What is he frightened of? Is he trying to protect you? Your home? Your car? Is he nervous because he suffered a trauma in the past that caused him pain? Was he poorly socialized when he was a puppy, and doesn't understand that humans and other dogs pose little threat to him? If your dog has bitten a person or another dog seemingly without warning, he has probably learned in the past that growling was not enough to see off whatever is frightening him and he has gone "straight to bite" because it works.

The solution is slow exposure to the person, dog, or whatever it is that is causing the fear. Never answer aggression with aggression. You will make it worse. Desensitizing a dog to a fearful stimulus is a long, slow process. You have to gradually condition the dog that the presence of the stimulus he was wary of now makes good things happen to him. He gets delicious food, he plays his favorite game, or he chews his favorite bone whenever that scary thing is present. Gradually, he will begin to relax and his stress levels will fall. It may take weeks, even months. You will need the help of a qualified trainer who uses positive methods.

Even after this kind of treatment, it is very important to note that once a dog has bitten, he is quite likely to bite again if he is put into a stressful situation. It's up to you to manage your dog's environment so that he doesn't experience the stimulus again in the same way. Aggression is a complex behavior to understand and treat.

Make sure there is no underlying physical cause that is predisposing your dog to aggressive behavior. I was once called in to assess a Labrador who had been wrongly diagnosed as aggressive by a veterinary behaviorist. In fact, the dog was being given an antihistamine to treat his itching skin. One of the side effects of the drug was irritability. The dog also suffered painful swollen paws, and the drug used to manage that condition had similar side effects.

Problem: Your dog is scared of men with beards

You have a loving, friendly dog that accepts and greets all visitors to your home. Except, that is, men with beards. When he sees a beard, he cowers and barks, then goes away to crouch under the table. You used to joke about it, but it's getting to be a bit of a problem, not to mention an embarrassment. Your next-door neighbor has a beard, and so does your brother.

Solution: Teach your dog that good things happen around men with beards

I've already explained how you can prepare a dog for the arrival of a new baby by playing a tape of a baby crying (page 180). You can use a similar technique to get your dog over his fear of beards.

These desensitization methods work by treating the fear through a gradual exposure to it. You reward the dog when he is calm around the source of his fear. In this case, try putting on a false beard. Ask your friends to do the same. Praise and treat your dog every time he remains calm.

Other fears and phobias

Is your dog scared of the vet? Get yourself the same kind of coat that your vet wears, and reward your dog when he's calm around you and other people wearing the coat.

Is your dog scared of fireworks? Equip yourself with a sound effects tape. Play the tape very softly to start with, giving your dog lots of praise and a reward when he is calm. Gradually increase the volume, praising and treating each time he remains calm. If he gets agitated, go back a step and repeat.

Some dogs can be treated to overcome their fear of thunderstorms in this way, but for many it doesn't work. It is thought that dogs, particularly those with longer coats and those that live in homes that are carpeted, can feel the static electricity of a thunderstorm long before it arrives. This would give them little shocks, especially on a carpeted floor. This theory might explain why many dogs will go to a bathroom and hide behind the sink or toilet, where proximity to pipes would ground them and reduce the unpleasant sensations. If your dog has a bad fear of thunderstorms, he might require medication. Your vet will be able to advise you. Whatever happens, allow your dog to find his own safe place, whether this is the bathroom or a cupboard, and let him stay there. Don't force him out.

Always be sensitive to the fact that fears and phobias, whether they are the product of breeding or learned experience, need to be treated slowly and carefully. Be very patient and never force your dog. He is feeling a very real emotion.

Worker's Playtime
how to have fun with your dog

Your dog is your responsibility. His life literally depends on you. But he should never be a chore. Play increases the bond between you and your dog, and it's a good way for both of you to unwind.

When I am showing owners how to teach their dogs basic commands, usually they're very serious while we're covering commands such as "sit" and "stay." When we get to "roll over," things lighten up a lot. Suddenly, everyone laughs and it's all very playful. But training should be like that all the time.

We humans make a very clear distinction between work time and playtime. That's not true with dogs. If you keep training positive and fun, work can be a form of play for a dog. Be playful when you work with your dog, and you can work your dog through his play.

Most dogs are highly motivated by food, which is why food treats are so effective as rewards for good behavior or success in training. But food is not the only effective reward. Toys and games work really well as rewards, too. Making your dog work for what gives him the most pleasure keeps him mentally alert and stimulated.

Activities

Walking – or running in the park – is great for your dog. But it's not the only way to give your pet the exercise he needs. There is a wide range of other activities that combine physical exercise with specific tasks, so your dog is not only getting a good workout, he's also learning how to do new things at the same time.

Humans have bred dogs for centuries to carry out specific tasks for them. Go with the flow, and choose games and activities that reflect what is already in your dog's nature. I'm not just talking about teaching Retrievers to retrieve, I'm talking about activities such as scent-tracking for Bloodhounds, mock gun-dog trials for Pointers and Labradors, and mock sheepdog trials for Border Collies. Dogs bred specifically to work in water, such as the Chesapeake Bay Retriever, the Portuguese Water Dog, and the Newfoundland Water Spaniel, really enjoy swimming. These types of activities give you the chance to step up the training a notch or two and really stretch your dog.

Dogs are not dumb animals. They are capable of carrying out very sophisticated tasks. Just think what a guide dog can do. A guide dog is not born with those skills; he's trained to do them. If you draw the line at teaching your dog to sit, you'll never know what he might be capable of.

Agility classes

Small active dogs, such as Jack Russell Terriers, particularly enjoy agility classes. These consist of assault courses that present the dog with a number of different obstacles that he has to negotiate – planks to tip, hoops to jump through, tunnels to race along, and that kind of thing. It's great exercise and very stimulating for the dog's mental powers, too.

Fly ball

This is another competitive activity that is very suitable for active working dogs such as Collies. It presents the dog with a number of jumps that he has to tackle before he reaches a platform, where he is trained to depress a pedal to release a ball. Then he has to bring the ball back to his owner.

Games

A good all-purpose game to play with your dog or puppy is hide-and-seek. You can play this game with your dog to reinforce your training of the "come" command. Hide yourself somewhere in the house and call your dog to "come" to you. Give him lots of praise and a reward when he finds you.

You can also hide food treats or hide part of his dinner in different places around the kitchen or his regular feeding area to make him work for his food. This isn't cruel. Dogs have to work for their food in the wild, and playing this game once in a while gives your dog extra sensory stimulation.

A refinement of hide-and-seek is the shell game. You hide a treat under one of three pots or overturned cups, shuffle them around, and get the dog to sniff out the treat with his nose. You can teach him to indicate the right pot or cup with his paw.

Another good game is chasing. Dogs are predisposed to chase moving things; it's how they track down their prey. Play chasing games in the garden. Get your dog to chase you – it's a great way of letting off steam. But stop the game if you spot the signs that your dog is getting over-excited. Never tease a dog when you are playing a chasing game – or any other time, for that matter.

Tug-of-war is another popular dog game, with dogs, that is. There is a lot of discussion about whether you should play this game with a dog. Some people believe it makes a dog aggressive and more prone to guarding his toys. Others believe that it provides a good bonding experience for dog and owner, and is a great way for the dog to release energy. I believe both. I like to play tug with a dog because it is great as a reward and it's an effortless way to exercise the dog. But I wouldn't continue with the game if the dog showed signs of becoming over-stimulated by it. And I always play the game in a controlled environment and with a proper tug rope that can withstand the considerable pressure of a dog's jaws.

I set up rules for the game. I will play tug with a dog as long as whenever I say "drop it," the dog drops the tug rope and surrenders his hold over it. The reward that I give him for this is another game of tug. Growling and over-excitement stop the game completely.

Play is a great way for both you
and your dog to unwind.

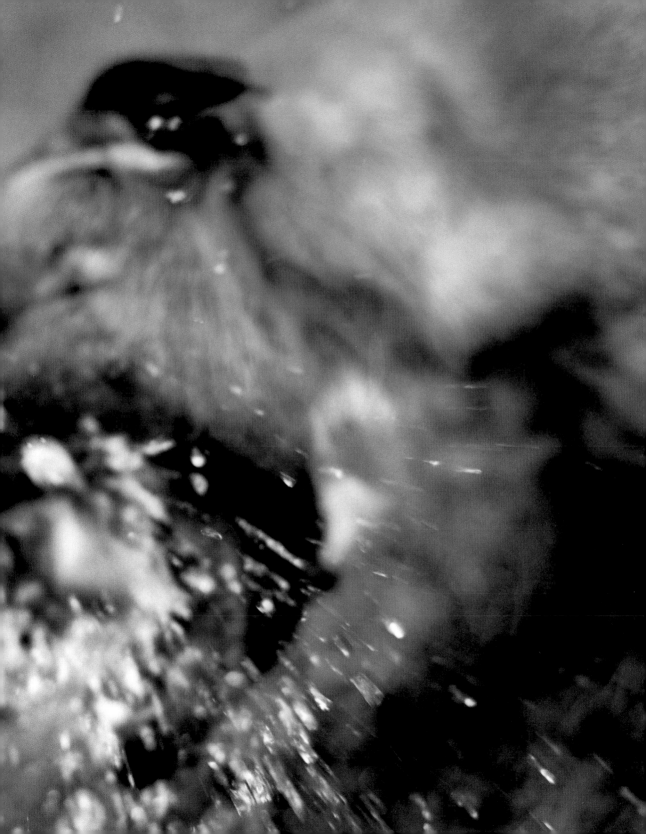

Toys

The best toys for dogs are both indestructible and interactive.
Indestructible toys are made of very hard rubber that does not break
into fragments.

Stuffed toys

Stuffed toys are OK, but they require
supervision because dogs can easily rip up the
material and eat the stuffing. Nothing that can
be chewed to pieces or ripped apart should
ever be left with an unsupervised dog.

Rubber toys

My favorites are those rubber toys that come in
different shapes and have holes in them. They
are an excellent way of keeping a dog happy
and busy for hours, especially when you have to
go out. I fill the toy with different things – peanut
butter or chicken – and pop it in the freezer for a
couple of hours, before giving it to the dog. This
makes the stuffing last longer and gives the
dog a good feeling on his gums. It's also an
excellent way to help puppies cope with
teething. In addition to the physical sensation,
the dog has to use his brain to figure out how
to get all those tasty treats out of the toy.

The cube

The cube is also a big favorite. Fill the cube with
your dog's dry food or treats, and watch him try
to get the food out by pushing the cube along
the floor with his nose.

Squeaking toys

Squeaking toys are also good fun. If you are in
any doubt about whether your dog would enjoy
making a toy squeak, give him a squeaky bone
for a while and then check out which end of it
has seen the most use!

Other toys

Toys such as Frisbees or the ever-popular
tennis ball are a good way of throwing a little
extra exercise into the picture. You get to stand
still and the dog has a good run back and forth.
Make sure you have taught your dog to "fetch"
first, or you may find he runs after the ball and
then takes it off somewhere where he can have
a quiet chew. Dogs can make short work of
tennis balls.

Tricks

Some people think that teaching dogs to do tricks is demeaning in some way for the animal. But as far as the dog is concerned, being asked to "sit" is no different than being asked to "roll over." They're both commands. Teaching your dog to do tricks is just an extension of basic obedience training. It also strengthens the bond between you because you are working and playing together.

Before you teach your dog a new trick, think about his anatomy and physical characteristics. Great Danes are too big to roll over. Dogs with bad hips should not be asked to sit for ages in order that you can teach them to give their paw.

Make training fun for your dog. Quick sessions, about five to ten minutes long, three times a day, are better than more protracted ones.

How to teach your dog to give his paw

I prefer to use the command "shake" rather than "paw." The gesture I use to accompany the command is a cupped hand.

Here's what you should do:

 Put your dog into a sit and place a treat on his nose.

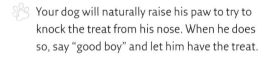 Your dog will naturally raise his paw to try to knock the treat from his nose. When he does so, say "good boy" and let him have the treat.

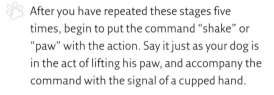 After you have repeated these stages five times, begin to put the command "shake" or "paw" with the action. Say it just as your dog is in the act of lifting his paw, and accompany the command with the signal of a cupped hand.

 Repeat these stages five more times.

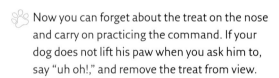 Now you can forget about the treat on the nose and carry on practicing the command. If your dog does not lift his paw when you ask him to, say "uh oh!," and remove the treat from view.

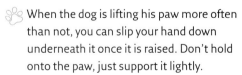 When the dog is lifting his paw more often than not, you can slip your hand down underneath it once it is raised. Don't hold onto the paw, just support it lightly.

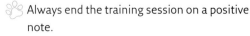 Always end the training session on a positive note.

How to teach your dog to roll over

This is a trick you can teach a dog once he has mastered the "down" command. The hand signal for this command is a circling finger.

Here's what you should do:

- Put your dog in a sit and then give him the "down" command.

- Crouch down beside your dog, right by his head, and place a treat beside his nose.

- Circle the treat over his nose.

- The dog will naturally roll over as he tries to follow the treat.

- When he rolls over, say "good boy," and give him the treat.

- After you have repeated these stages five times, begin to put the command "roll over" with the action. Say it just as your dog is in the act of rolling over, and accompany the command with the signal of a circling finger.

- Repeat these stages five more times.

- Now you can start to ask him to "roll over" without circling the treat around his nose. Praise and reward him when he gets it right. When he doesn't, say "uh oh!," and remove the treat from view.

- End each session on a positive note.

Teaching your dog to do tricks is just an extension of basic obedience training.

You don't need fancy equipment
to train a dog. You need time
and patience – and a sense of fun!

How to teach your dog to fetch

You're going with the flow if you teach your Retriever to fetch, because that's what these dogs are bred to do. But even Retrievers won't retrieve if what you are throwing for them is not worth fetching. There are many ways to teach a dog to fetch, but this is one of my favorites.

Here's what you should do:

Start by showing your dog a toy or some other object that he likes, but that is not too valuable to him to be given up.

As soon as your dog puts his mouth over the toy, ask him to "take it."

Play with your dog for a while.

After a couple of minutes, ask the dog to drop the toy into your hand, using the "drop it" command.

When he releases the toy, praise him.

Then throw the toy on the ground a small distance away. As soon as he puts his mouth on it, say "take it," and praise him again.

Then it's playtime again.

After a few minutes, ask your dog to drop the toy, using the "drop it" command. He should drop the toy into your hand. When he does, praise him and reward him.

Repeat the sequence, throwing the toy greater distances each time you play the game. That's what it is, one big game!

When your dog is good at playing the game, use toys or objects of higher value and that are, therefore, more stimulating to retrieve.

You can teach an old dog new tricks. And you should. Keep teaching and training your dog all through his life. Vary the picture with different routines, rewards, and games.

Playtime problems

The biggest problem that most dogs have with play is that there is just not enough of it in their lives. A really good play session is worth a million walks (not that you should use that as an excuse to skip the trip to the park!). Have fun with your dog. It's good for both of you.

Problem: Toy guarding

Your dog has a favorite squeaky bone. He won't let anyone near it. If you try to get the bone so you can play a game of fetch, he growls at you.

Solution: Be the keeper of your dog's toys

Remember that toys are one of a dog's resources. They are very precious to him. Toy guarding is common, particularly when there are two dogs in the home, in which case the guarding might well lead to fighting.

The solution is to remember who is top dog. That's you. You have to be the source of your dog's toys. Don't allow him to have the toy that encourages the guarding behavior. Take charge of all his toys and give them out to him as rewards in training sessions. Make him work for his pleasurable experiences.

Useful Contacts

American Kennel Club
Information on breeds, breeders, clubs, activities, healthcare plans, and all aspects of dog ownership.
www.akc.org

American Veterinary Medical Association
Listing of accredited behavioral counselors.
www.avma.org

American Veterinary Medical Association: Care for Pets
Advice on pet health, choosing a dog, safety, first aid, and choosing a vet.
www.avma.org/care4pets

ASPCA
American Society for the Prevention of Cruelty to Animals. Information on pet care, nutrition, campaigns against animal cruelty, publications, and legal advice.
www.aspca.org

Association of Pet Behaviour Counsellors
International network of qualified counselors treating problem behaviors in pet animals.
www.apbc.org.uk

Association of Pet Dog Trainers
An organization that provides lists of trainers that train using positive methods.
www.apdt.co.uk

Dog Trainers of New York
Advice on obedience training and behavior modification.
www.dogtrainersofnewyork.com

Greyhound Pets of America
Nationwide charity dedicated to adopting ex-racing dogs.
www.greyhoundpets.org

Humane Society of the United States
Charity dedicated to helping pet animals and wildlife.
www.hsus.org

Petfinder.com
Adopt a pet dog or cat from animal welfare organizations across the country.
www.petfinder.com

Pet Health Care
Comprehensive online source of pet care information. Guide to breeds. Pet insurance. Online veterinary advice.
www.PEThealthcare.co.uk

Pets 911
Information on the location of animal shelters. Adoptions and lost animals.
www.pets911.com

Stray from the Heart
Nonprofit rescue organization that rescues, rehabilitates, and re-homes homeless dogs.
www.strayfromtheheart.org

Index

Acknowledgments

There are so many people that have made this book possible and I want to thank them all. First, I thank my parents, who worked so hard to give me the best in life: my late father, Malcolm Stilwell, who would have been so proud, and my mother, Vernie Stilwell, who taught me that passion and determination go hand in hand. Thanks to my sister, Nicola, who gave me the idea that dog-walking was a really fun way to make a living, and to my brother-in-law, Alan, for always making sure that I don't take myself too seriously. To my late grandmother, Estelle Hepworth, who taught me to respect and care for all animals. A million thanks to my in-laws, Rita and Van, for their unwavering support and wisdom and to all my family across the pond.

I am blessed with a wonderful family both in England and America.

Thank you also to my great friends. To Alex, Monica, and Nathan, who remind me why I love England so much, and Helen and Elio, who fill our lives with music and a lot of laughs! To Catherine and Tim (you have been such a great support), and to Emily, who has taught me what it is to be strong in the face of adversity. To Cathy, Alistair, and Thomas, who show me why friendship can be such a pleasure.

Then to those who have been responsible for my learning. To Ken Cockram, an inspirational trainer, who gave me valuable insight into the canine world, and to my training partner, Garry Gross, who helped me develop my passion and keeps me on my toes. To Dr. Berman of Park East Animal Hospital in NYC for believing in me.

Many thanks to the people who made the television series *It's Me or the Dog* happen.

To all the outstanding and vibrant team at Ricochet. It has been wonderful to work with you. To Channel 4 for believing in this project. Thanks to my agents Geraldine Woods and Jon Roseman – how lucky I am to have found such great support. To Liz Wilhide, Denise Bates, and all those at Collins, to Smith and Gilmour for their brilliant design, and to Mark Read for his wonderful photography. To all those at Hyperion for believing in this. It has been such fun to work with you on this book and thank you for making sense of my scrawl. Thank you to all the families that took part in the program and who opened up their homes to us. Respect to you all.

And last, but by no means least, thanks to all the dogs that have come into my life. You have taught me everything that I know and you have inspired me by your unwavering loyalty and trust. You make the world a better place and I am dedicated to making it a better place for you, too.

The publishers would like to thank the following for kindly allowing us to feature their dogs: A–Z Animals and Brakabreeze Hawke (Trog) and Tara, Louise Dyer and Alfie, Jinnie Chalton Ena and Tosca, Brian Foster and Lizzie, Jacqui Hurst and Digby, Bryony James and Barney, Emma Johnson and Bella, Michael Ruggins and Max, Alex Smith and Jess, Marcia Stanton and Doris and Jo-Jo, Fiona Worthington and Pepper, and Marcus Yorke and Loopy.

The publishers would like to thank the Mayhew Animal Home and Pet Planet (www.petplanet.co.uk tel: 0845 345 0723) for supplying props for photography.